My Father and Edward Ardizzone

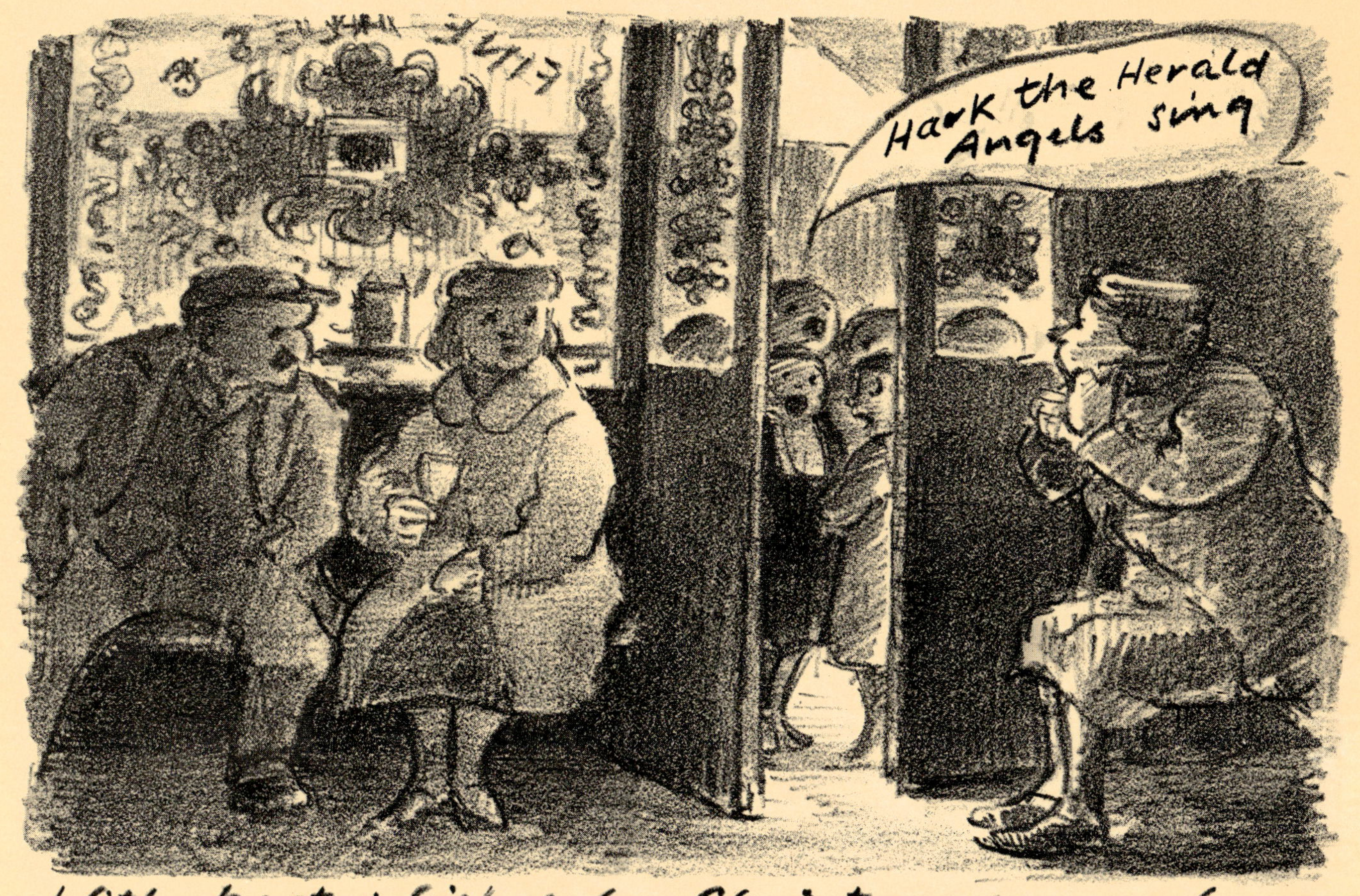

With best Wishes for Christmas —— from
Catherine & Edward Ardizzone
To Helen & Augustus, With love   Xmas 1966

My Father and Edward Ardizzone

A Lasting Friendship

By Edward Booth-Clibborn · Illustrated with Ardizzone Christmas cards

PATRICK HARDY BOOKS · LONDON

PATRICK HARDY BOOKS
28 Percy Street
London W1P 9FF
UK

Designed by Gerald Cinamon
First published in 1983
by Patrick Hardy Books

ISBN 0 7444 0018 X

Photoset in Linotron Aldus by
Rowland Phototypesetting Limited
Printed in Great Britain

For CHARLES
PATRICK
JAMES

ACKNOWLEDGEMENTS: *I would very much like to thank a number of people who helped me prepare this book, especially Catherine Ardizzone for her reminiscences, Gabriel White for the loan of missing cards and for his encouragement, Hetti Einzig for her editorial advice and Jonathan and Phillida Gili whose original idea inspired the writing of this book.*

The author and publishers are grateful to the Bodley Head for allowing them to quote a passage from Gabriel White's book Edward Ardizzone.

Nowadays we take Christmas cards for granted. Indeed many of us have stopped sending them altogether. And yet they are still an important and often much appreciated mark of affection to loved ones, to family and friends far away. Their meaning should not be under-estimated, especially for the elderly, the sick, and for children, who generally take immense pleasure in decorating the house with these bright seasonal messages of good will. We are inclined to think that the sending of cards at Christmas is a tradition that has been going for ages, but in fact it started only as far back as the last century, at around the same time as the Christmas tree was introduced to this country. And whereas there has been a celebration at this low point in the winter since the earliest times, it was only officially adopted by the Christian religions relatively late; the first use of the word Christmas, for instance, is recorded as being in 1594.

Many illustrators and painters have produced their own Christmas cards but none have drawn so consistently and so vividly from their immediate surroundings and family – from the apparently unpicturesque and everyday – for their seasonal greetings as did the painter-illustrator Edward Ardizzone.

Edward Ardizzone, internationally known for the children's books he illustrated and for the series he created relating the adventures of Tim, was for the greater part of his life a close friend of my father, Augustin Booth-Clibborn, who was himself also a painter.

They met at the Westminster School of Art (officially known as the Westminster Technical Institute) where they were both studying, and became close companions until my father left London to live and work in Broadstairs. From then on, apart from regular visits from Ted, and the visits of my father to Elgin Avenue, my father received annually an Ardizzone Christmas card. These cards became for my mother and father cherished pictorial reminders of the London they had left and the intimate quality that Ardizzone instinctively put into them gave them a special value for all his friends.

Edward Ardizzone was born in Haiphong, in the province of Tonkin, China, on October 16th 1900. His father, Augustin, was an Italian by birth who spent his working life in the Far East. His mother, Margaret Irving, was half Scots and half English, and was a keen amateur water colourist; she studied drawing at the Atelier Colarossi in Paris during the 1880's and must have rubbed shoulders with many of the great artists of the period. Edward had two sisters, Betty and Tetta and two younger brothers, David and Michael.

The family came to Britain in 1905 and lived in various parts of England before settling for a time in Ipswich and then Wokingham. After this move Edward went to a public school called Clayesmore, at that time near the river Thames at Pangbourne. In 1918 the family moved to Bath. Edward's first job was in Warminster and then in London where he boarded with his grandmother. In 1920 the whole family moved to London and set up home at 130 Elgin Avenue, in Maida Vale; this remained the Ardizzone family home for 52 years. It was a large Victorian terraced house on three floors with a balcony over the front door – ideal for the extended family that Augustin, following in the Italian tradition, had planned. It is a solid house built of red brick and portland stone with a slate roof, and it is still today covered with the soot of industrial London.

In 1921 Edward got a job in the city as a clerk in the statistical department of the Eastern Telegraph Company. It was at this time that he started attending evening classes three times a week at the Westminster School of Art.

Here he met people who were to have an influence on his life – among them Freddie Mayor, the art dealer, and Walford Crampton Chalk, a director of *Technical Advertising*, who also studied drawing at the Westminster and was later to give Ardizzone one of his first jobs. Gabriel White was also studying painting there and later married Edward's sister Betty.

It was in 1928, at one of the regular dances held at the Westminster, that Gabriel and Betty decided to announce their engagement. The dance was a fancy dress affair and Edward and Gabriel dressed as costers. This was the night that Edward met his future wife, Catherine Anderson. Dressed in a Spanish shawl she had gone to the dance with an artist called Medworth and his family. Catherine recalls the occasion: 'I had an enormous Spanish shawl. We became part of their party and then we discovered that we lived just round from Ted in Blomfield Road – so after that we saw a lot of them. And finally Ted and I got married.' The pair were married at the Jesuit church in St. John's Wood, Our Lady of Victories, on April 2nd 1929 and thereupon became heads of the family home at Elgin Avenue.

It was during this time that my father met Ardizzone. Both of them were studying under the renowned Bernard Meninsky at the Westminster Technical Institute in Vincent Square. Bernard Meninsky was a painter well-known for his strong figure drawing and it can be clearly seen that he was a formative influence on the Ardizzone style, imparting his use of line and his love of the well-made female form.

Meninsky had taken over from Walter Sickert as tutor at the Westminster and was influential both as a teacher and as a painter in his own right. His method of teaching was by example, drawing small studies and explanatory sketches at the side of the student's own work. He was always encouraging his students, both during classes and afterwards, talking to them about draughtsmanship, classical painting and the French Impressionists.

My father was older than Ardizzone and had an entirely different temperament. Perhaps it was a case of the attraction of opposites – in any case they took to each other and remained firm friends for life.

My father was born in Paris in 1892 with the name Arthur Augustin Booth-Clibborn. He painted under the name of Augustin Booth, his reason being, so he told me, that he wanted to be known in his own right as an artist, and not as the grandson of the famous General Booth, founder of the Salvation Army, and, more particularly, as the eldest son of the well-known Evangelist preacher Mrs. Booth-Clibborn, known as 'La Maréchale', who founded the 'Army' in France. My father even later tried to persuade me to change my name by dropping the Clibborn and retaining only the more anonymous Booth. And such was La Maréchale's reputation that even my aunt, Nina Hamnett, also a painter, and not a blood relation, felt the same way about the family connection!

Although born in Paris, my father studied in Germany. He was a good linguist and spoke fluent French and German, the former, however, with a German accent; this was to cause him serious problems. Having been born in France he was called up to serve in the 1914–18 war in the French army but his German accent led to him being picked up several times as a possible spy. Invalided out of the army for shell shock he considered a number of different careers before deciding that painting was his vocation in life. He then spent some time in Paris where he became a friend of Modigliani's. In a typically extravagant gesture one day my father gave him his splendid great coat. In Paris my father moved in artistic and eccentric circles and at one time crossed paths, as it were, with the notorious sorcerer Aleister Crowley.

Back in London he lived in Highgate and became a friend of the composer, Peter Warlock (whose real name was Philip Heseltine) and soon made his mark as a flamboyant figure in the London art scene. He was a friend of Augustus John, of Vivian Locke Ellis, the poet, the notorious Betty May, the Tiger Woman, and of Nina Hamnett, who introduced him to her sister, Helen, whom my father later married. He also met Ivor Novello and they worked together on an opera score. During this same period my father was lecturing at the Wallace Collection and the National Gallery as well as writing poems, articles – and of course, painting.

Catherine Ardizzone reminded me recently that it was my father who urged and encouraged Edward to take up drawing professionally. My father was well-known to have a good eye for talent and he thought very highly of Edward's gifts as an artist. Older than Ardizzone he also had a strong personality and was outspoken and generous in his praise of the younger man. This no doubt helped Edward to take the plunge and in 1927 to give up his steady job at the Eastern Telegraph Company – very much against his father's wishes – for the precarious life of an artist.

Catherine recalls the flavour of those early years with Edward when there was no regular income, and often no work for him of any kind. Once the children were old enough, 'I used to go out and get temporary typing. I found an Irish girl, Margaret, who used to come in the morning at 9.00, give the children their lunch, take them for a walk in the afternoon, and give them tea – all this for £1 a week! Ted was at home all day long and then he slowly started getting things. He sold a picture for £3 and he nearly fainted. Then he got work at the Radio Times and then Peter Davies gave him *In a Glass Darkly* to illustrate and that really made him feel he was getting somewhere.' Later he looked on this as one of his best books.

As Edward was a shy young man he enjoyed my father's company. Extrovert and ebullient, my father was Edward's introduction to the art world. Its social centre at that time was the Fitzroy Tavern in Charlotte Street, Soho, otherwise known, after its proprietor, as Kleinfelds. They would also go drinking together on Edward's home ground, in the large and beautiful pubs around Maida Vale.

Around 1929 my father moved into a studio on the top floor of the Vale of Health Hotel. Also a pub, it had a large veranda which was a great attraction: on a summer evening it was a pleasant place to sit with a drink enjoying the view over the Hampstead Ponds.

Next to the pub was a fairground, which is still there today, despite the pub having long since been replaced with the grey slab of an apartment block.

Stanley Spencer had a studio there in 1923–1927 and it was here that he painted part of *The Resurrection of Cookham*. The sections had to be lowered down from the windows because the stairs were too narrow. His well-known painting *The Roundabout* was also painted there.

Catherine recalls my father's studio: 'It was wonderful with windows all round; very empty with lots of canvas lying around and a large table to eat off and a kitchen where your mother would make wonderful meals. A great deal of merry-making went on!'

Ardizzone would often come to paint landscape sketches on the Heath near the pub. One day, on their way across the Heath to the Vale of Health, he and Gabriel met my father. As they approached he looked up from his painting and announced: 'I have just got married'! In spite of their close friendship this was the first they heard of his wedding!

I was born in this studio in 1932. The people who owned the pub were an old circus family called Gray and my father told me that the elderly grandmother was a woman boxer who acted as the bouncer removing the many boisterous late drinkers. Indeed there was always plenty going on and many artists and writers frequented the place, including Augustus John. My father's studio was quite a focal point and Catherine remembers the many happy hours that they spent there. 'Your mother always had something to give away. She gave me some beautiful dresses and lovely baby clothes, hand-embroidered by some relation. I gave them all back again – but I don't think she meant me to!'

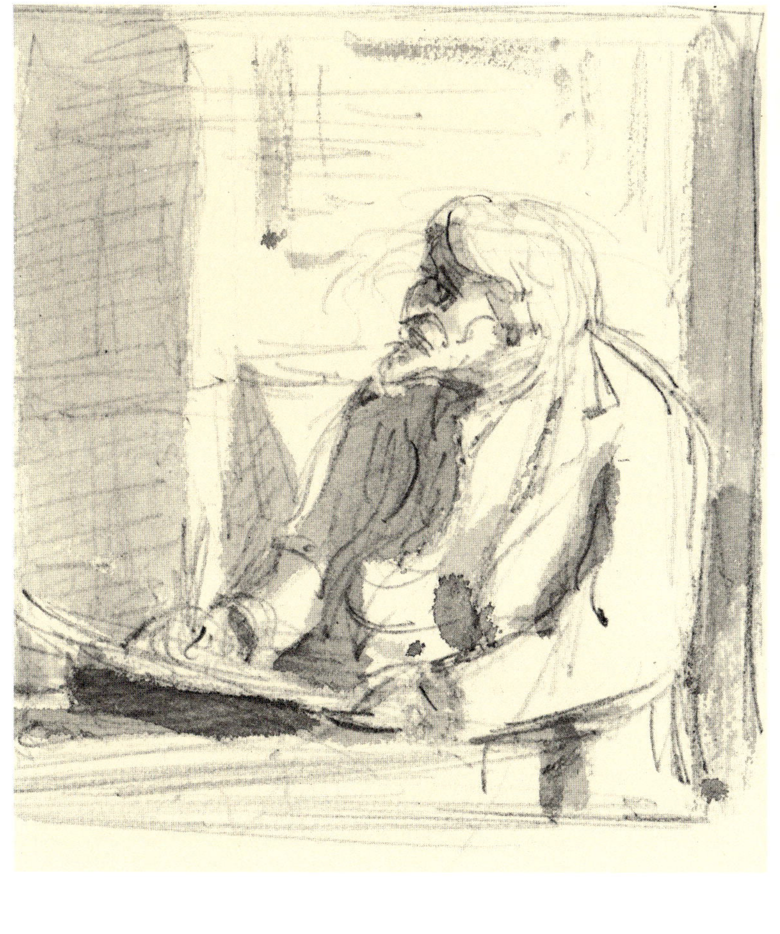

Augustin Booth: a quick drawing by Edward Ardizzone

My father and Ted often worked together. As with teaching, each gained a lot from seeing the other at work. It wasn't always harmonious though. Catherine describes one incident that sticks in her mind: 'Once they both decided they were going to paint a portrait of me. So there I sat in a shiny black dress and it lasted exactly one morning. Finally your father said, ''I can't bear it any more.'' He looked at Ted. ''I know I'm irritating you beyond endurance. I can't stand here and paint with you in the same room.'' And that was the end of that.'

In 1932 my father had a one-man show at the Bloomsbury Gallery. Later my family left the Vale of Health and moved briefly to a studio in Barnes. Then in 1936 we all moved to Bradstow Way, Broadstairs. Queen Victoria had a house there and it was a favourite watering place of Winston Churchill's as well. There my father took over Walter Sickert's studio in Kings Avenue for a short time. Sickert himself lived in St. Peter's, a nearby village, until 1939, and taught at the Margate School of Art which is where I eventually started my art training.

The bungalow style studio had been built at about that time and had a small garden all round it. Dividing it from the road was a six foot high wooden fence on which Sickert had painted in large white letters: WALTER SICKERT, MEMBRE DU SALON FRANCAIS. After the war, someone creosoted over the letters and cut the fence down to three feet – and you can still see the absurd sight of some of the white lettering showing through the creosote coating!

From the time of our departure from London my father and Ardizzone corresponded regularly, exchanging their views on painting techniques amongst other things. I remember well Ardizzone's visits to Broadstairs after the war when, as a child, I would watch him leave the house with my father, deep in conversation, for their now famous lunches at Marchesi's Restaurant with its fine view overlooking Viking Bay. To this day, the Rogers' family, the owners of the restaurant, recall the boisterous four-hour lunches that the pair passed in Marchesi's. These meetings became a regular twice yearly event, ending only when Edward could no longer travel easily in his later years. They would talk of old times and painting and my father would express his satisfaction and delight at Ardizzone's great success.

THE CHRISTMAS CARDS

Christmas, as for any young person, was an important time of the year for me. Christmas cards were not many in our family but the card from Catherine and Edward every year had a special meaning for us. It brought to us Ardizzone's sense of humour, his warmth and his observations of London. The cards created for us a yearly visual record of the far-off city seen through his eyes. It was not the bright lights of the capital that we got to know from the cards but the local life of Maida Vale, one of the many villages that make up London.

The first known Christmas card that Ardizzone drew was in 1932. It shows him and his wife Catherine with their first two children, Christianna and Philip, and the cat, Francis.

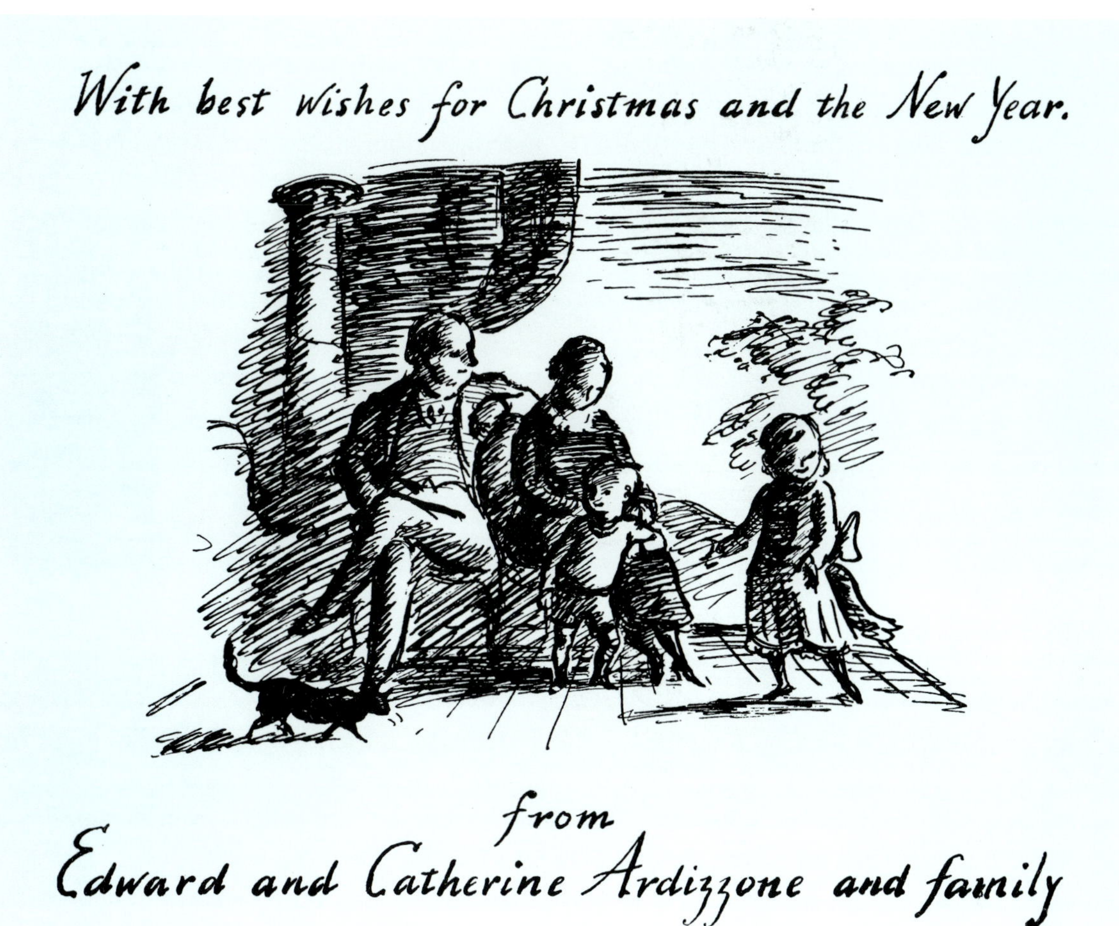

Catherine comments on the start of this annual production: 'He *must* have done one every year – he would never have dreamt of *buying* a Christmas card!'

In these early days only 20 copies of each card were produced, mainly for family and close friends.

The card of 1938 was the first Ardizzone did using lithography. It is not very successful if one compares it with the cards of the 1950's. He was at this time much happier with pen and ink. This card is interesting also as it is the first one depicting the interior of a pub.

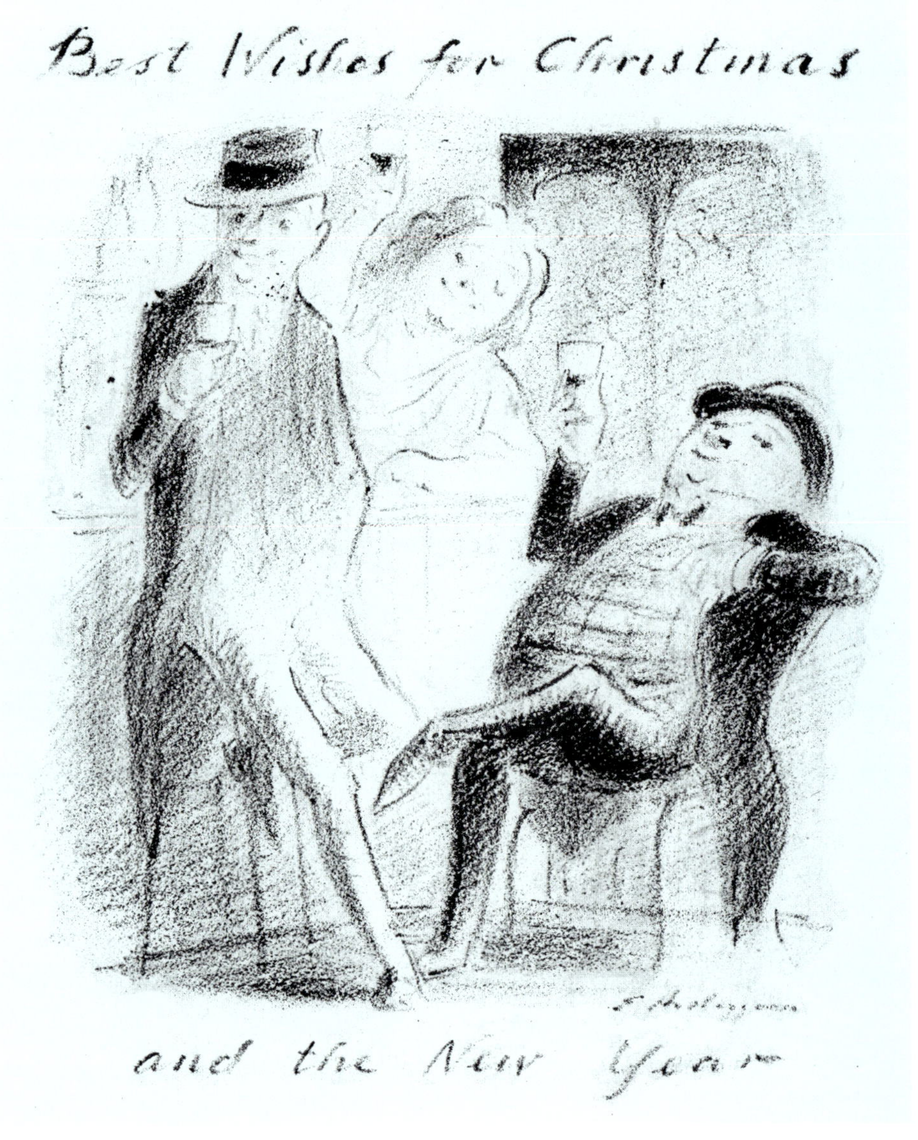

Best Wishes for Christmas
and the New Year

The card of 1939 shows Christmas Eve in the Warrington Hotel. It captures the bright pre-war atmosphere of bustling warmth in those huge Edwardian Maida Vale public houses, which was rather different to that of pubs in other areas of London [see p. 15].

Maida Vale is an exclusively residential area of spacious nineteenth century stucco houses between the Harrow Road and the Regent's Canal. It was a much livelier part of London than it appears today. The canal, built in 1820 to link the Grand Junction Canal with the Thames at Limehouse to form the Grand Union, was a fully working trade route until well after the Second World War. The area had good bus services to the centre of the city and, in those days, a large community of artists, actors and writers who would all congregate in one or other of the many noisy, warm pubs that formed the social centres of the district.

These public houses are particularly fine examples of Victorian and Edwardian pub architecture and the ornately carved and mirrored interiors of such pubs as the Warrington, on the corner of Warrington Crescent and Sutherland Avenue, and the Prince Alfred in Formosa Street can still be found looking exactly the same today, mercifully protected from modernization by preservation orders.

In his book on Ardizzone, Gabriel White has captured in suitably rotund style the *louche* plushness and faded grandeur of these pubs – as well as their relaxed, friendly atmosphere – during the period when Ardizzone was a regular.

More grandiose is the Warrington Hotel . . . with its monumental circular bar and grand staircase which seems to invite to greater splendour upstairs. It was here that a battered oil painting used to hang, an indifferent copy of *Rape of Europa*. From darkness and decay however its story, though appropriate, could have said little to those who passed it by. The whole saloon was resplendent with mirrors and gilded stucco ornament, and even the tables, with beaten copper tops, glittered at all times of day. Ardizzone lost no opportunities here. We see 'the girls', who were all respectability when having their evening drink, and the constant procession on the stairs. The waiter with his sad aged face, once a Brighton choirboy, can be recognized in the Christmas festivities.

At other pubs customers were tougher and more demonstrative and tastes and decorations were flashier, or there were the many little quiet respectable houses where the landlord or landlady was a character and there was a family feeling among the customers. It was these that best provided the small emotional and psychological situations which Ardizzone observed and depicted so sensitively [p. 16].

It is clear that the various pubs of Maida Vale, with their different atmospheres and clientele, were central to a whole body of Ardizzone's work, and not just a chance subject for a Christmas card. The card of 1949, for instance, shows how faithfully he reproduced the ornate interiors of the pubs he loved; this card comes from a book he did on local pubs. Later on, when I visited the Ardizzones and Edward took me along with him for a drink, I was impressed by the conviviality and warmth of the red plush upholstered interiors. The dark varnished mahogany bars and panels and the sparkling, engraved glass and mirrors, already familiar from the cards we had been receiving over the years in Broadstairs, came vividly to life for me. I felt also

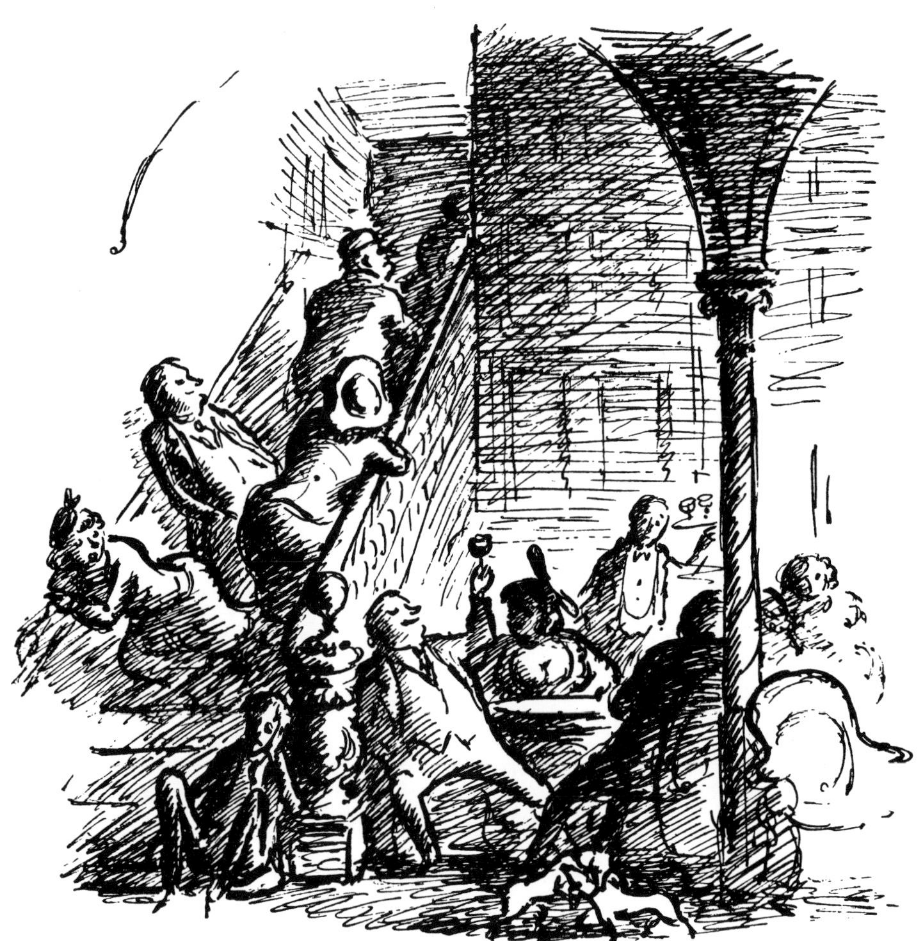

Christmas Eve at the Warrington

Best wishes for Christmas
and the New Year from
Catherine + Edward Ardizzone.

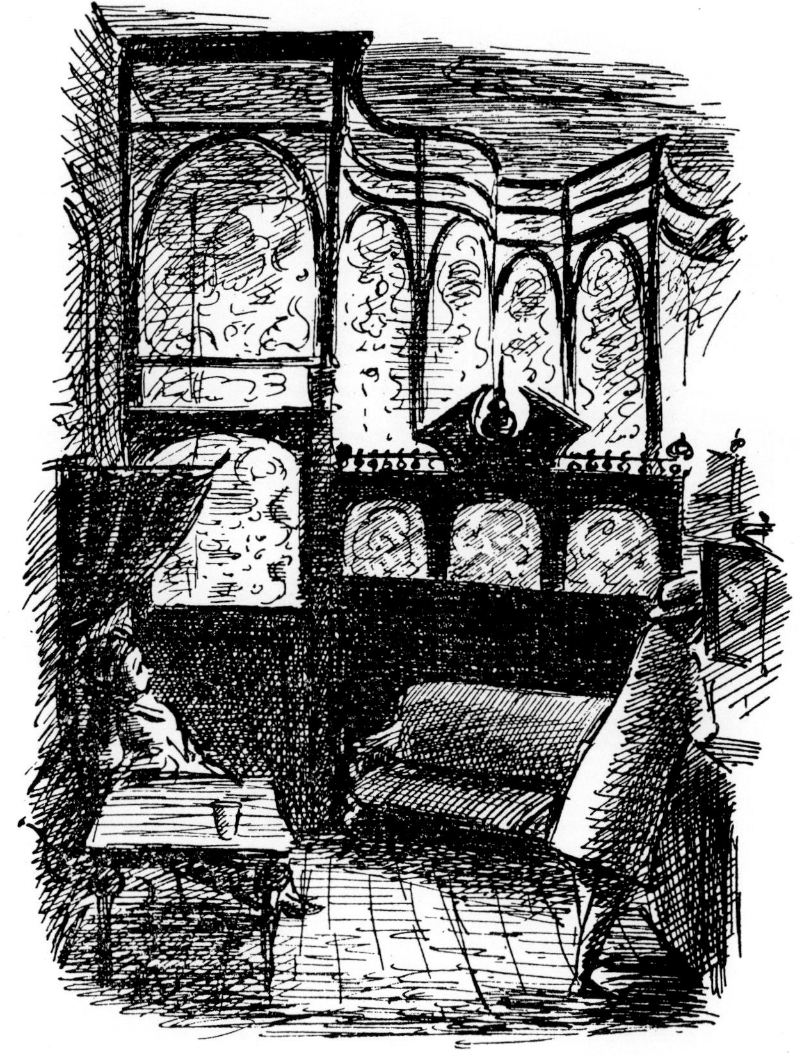

The Saloon Bar at the Prince
Alfred

that I was an intruder into a special world. Not just because I was a young boy, and possibly tiresome to the crowd of drinking adults, but because these pubs and the people who frequented them with unfailing loyalty, represented a particular society and a way of life that was close, comfortable and secure and that belonged to that pre-war era and which would never be repeated.

At the outbreak of war Ardizzone served in the territorial anti-aircraft regiment and it was not until early 1940 that he became an official war artist. In March of that year he went to France and at Christmas he drew a card of the regiment he was attached to at Merris. He then returned to London where he recorded the effects of the blitz until 1942 [p. 18].

Despite the war good cheer continues to reign in his Christmas cards.

His 1941 card shows some of the Ardizzone family in their Anderson shelter in the garden of Elgin Avenue. It depicts Edward, Gabriel White, his wife Betty, and Jane Creswell who was a lodger of Betty and Gabriel's and worked at Good Housekeeping. Catherine had taken the children to Montgomery in Wales: hence the leafy thought bubbles surrounding the shelter [p. 19].

The card was and still is a poignant one for me: I too spent Christmas in an Anderson shelter, in our garden in Broadstairs. The shelter had two bunks down each side and one across the bottom. I recall looking out on to a night full of smoke and fires and the whistle of falling bombs which seemed to last for an eternity till they hit the ground. And then returning quickly to the safety of the shelter for fear of falling shrapnel. My memories of that

austere candle-lit Christmas are still vivid, with my father, who was now in the ARP (Air Raid Precautions), being too old for active service, away on night watch.

From 1942 until the end of the war Ardizzone was in North Africa, Sicily and Europe, still as an official war artist, spending only his leave of 1944 in England. During his stay in Italy he made a Christmas card for his army unit, but this one has been lost.

During the war 130 Elgin Avenue was damaged several times and the house next door was destroyed. However, the family returned to their home in 1945 and in 1946, while repairs were being done to the house, Ardizzone set up his studio for the year in the basement of 88 Maida Vale, the home of a first cousin of his, Mary Lewis, better known as the writer, Christianna Brand.

I visited this studio on one of my trips up to London in the summer of 1946. Ted gave me a part of the studio to work in, sitting me down with paper and paints in a corner, and occasionally coming over to look at how I was getting on. At the time he was working on a lithograph for the Lyons Corner Tea Houses. Working in his studio gave me the opportunity to watch Ted at work on the litho stones which would be taken by Curwen Press to Camberwell School of Art to be printed. It was a series that Barnett Freedman also contributed to and they were put up in Lyons Corner Houses all over the country; I remember seeing them later in Margate when I was studying at the art school there.

It was during this time that he gave up using lithography as a medium for the main body of his art and used it only for Christmas cards. It is difficult, however, to date this

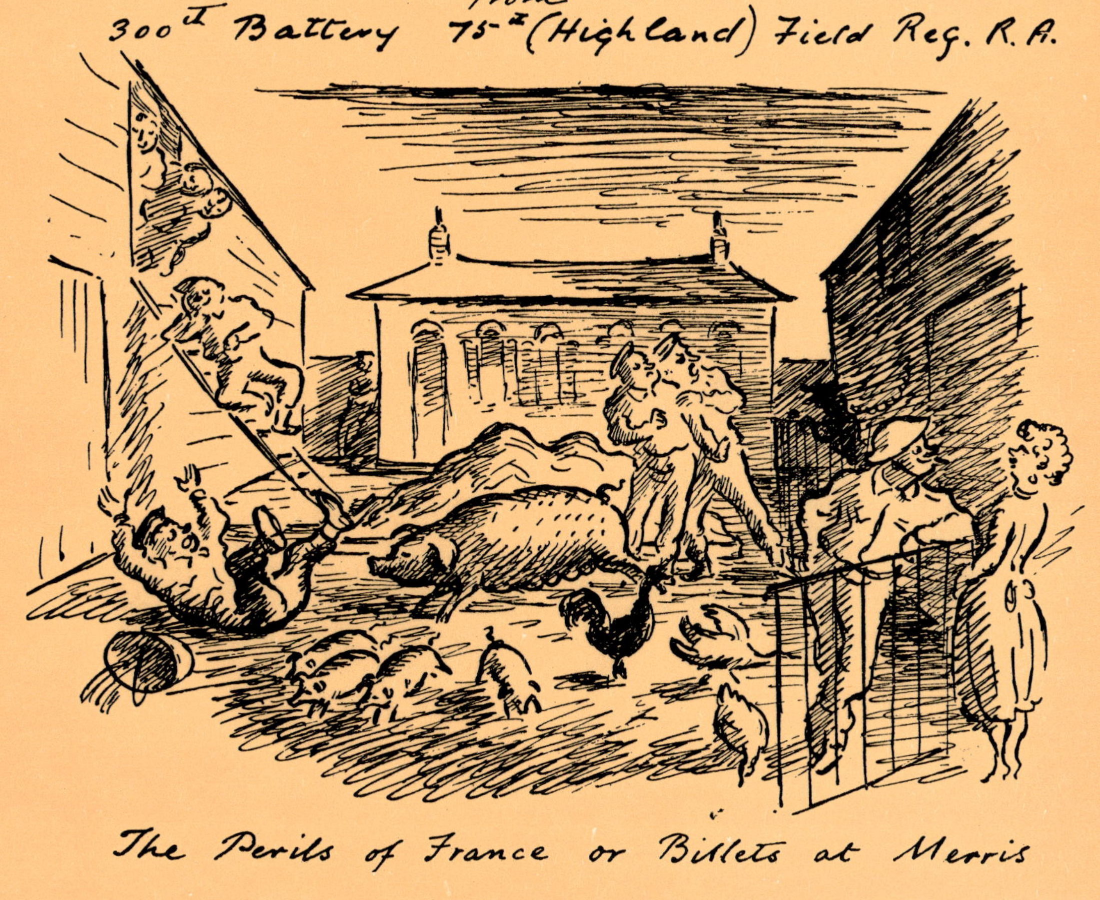

Best Wishes for Christmas & the New Year
from
300th Battery 75th (Highland) Field Reg. R.A.
The Perils of France or Billets at Merris

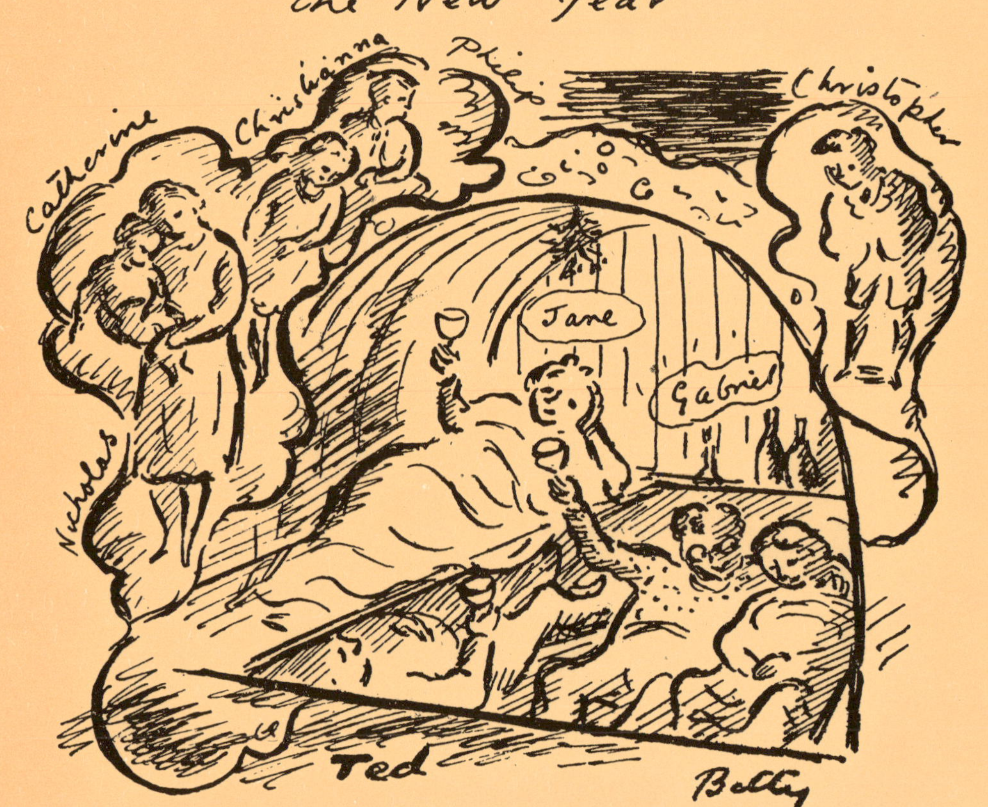

From the Ardizzones, Whiles,
and Jane Creswell
in the Anderson at —
130 Elgin Avenue, London W.9.

decision exactly since Ardizzone always refused to date any of his work. 'It'll be work for the art historians!' he would say gleefully with a mischievousness that delighted his friends but has exasperated subsequent collectors of his art.

The early cards were mostly pen and ink drawings and Edward would colour many of them by hand, some with a blue wash, some ochre, others green and so on. This would be done in between other things, when he and Catherine were, as she said, 'just sitting about and he was rather pleased with what he had done.' It soon became no mean task however, for he was quickly producing up to 200 copies of one card every year.

Another card of the Prince Alfred shows Ted himself joking with the bar-maid. The two women smiling indulgently round the banquette provide the constant reminder that he has been there a little too long. The dog in the foreground is 'Jock', who joined the family during the war and remained with them for fifteen years.

A Street at Dusk sums up the pre-Christmas London street scenes with the crush of last minute shoppers hurrying to get all done before the shops close. It reminds me of the frantic bustle of Christmas Eve. Bright lights from the warm pub emphasize the darkening sky and damp chill outside. The queue of people in the background is possibly for the cinema and the throng of people in the foreground outside the pub is typical of the scene outside many a London pub: friends from the office having a last drink before catching the bus home, laden with their parcels for the big day to follow. I remember my father coming home late on Christmas Eve with the turkey. He would always wait to buy till the very last minute knowing that he could pick up a bargain [p. 22]!

The next card shows another scene from the Ardizzone family life. Philip, to the left of the table, is now a young man, with beard and wine tasting skills and all! Looking on are Christianna and Nicholas, the Ardizzone's youngest son. Attempting to steal her dinner while the others are occupied with merry-making is one of the several Ardizzone cats [p. 23].

Apart from the Christmas cards Ardizzone was renowned among his friends for his illustrated letters, many of which would be sent during the festive season. But he never sent these illustrated letters to other artists – 'They do not need them' he would say. And indeed, of all the many letters he wrote to my father not one is illustrated.

The next card evokes well the damp, grimy cold of London under snow. But, as always, there is the light Ardizzone touch in the mischievous boys lying in wait with their snowballs and in the mangy mongrel treading daintily through the slush. The terrace of houses in the background is Elgin Avenue [p. 24].

Jock reappears in the following card curled snugly on the floor of the Alma. This was a pub in St. John's Wood that Edward and Catherine used to enjoy going to a lot. It was smaller and cosier than the Maida Vale showpieces and had a more regular and intimate social life [p. 25].

These cards all evoked memories in Broadstairs.

Best Wishes for Christmas & the New Year

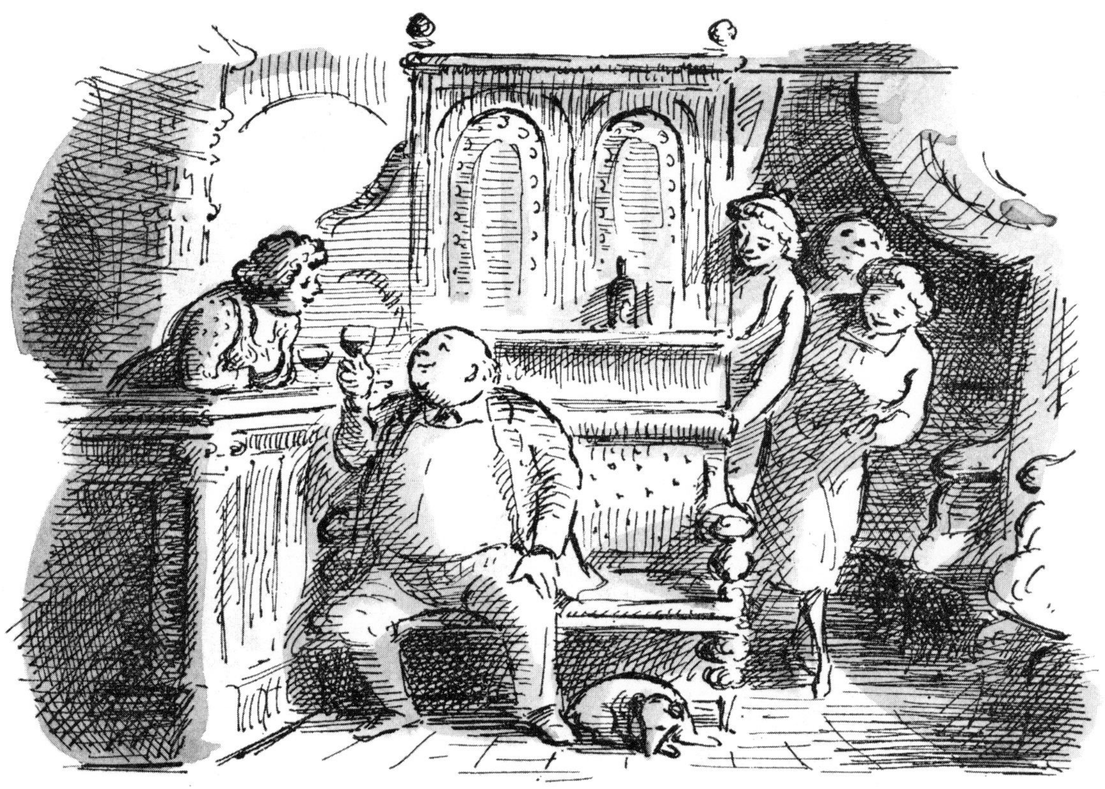

from Edward & Catherine Ardizzone

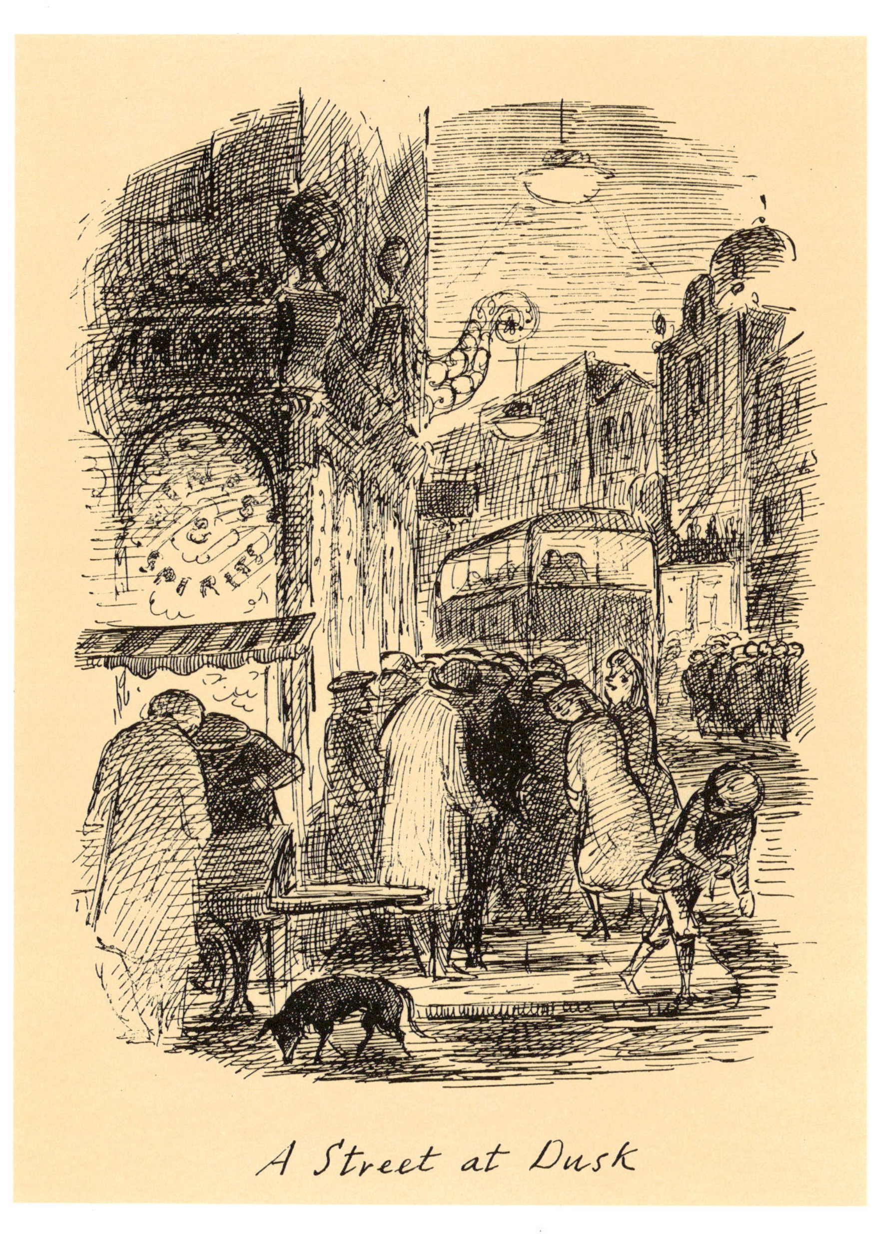

A Street at Dusk

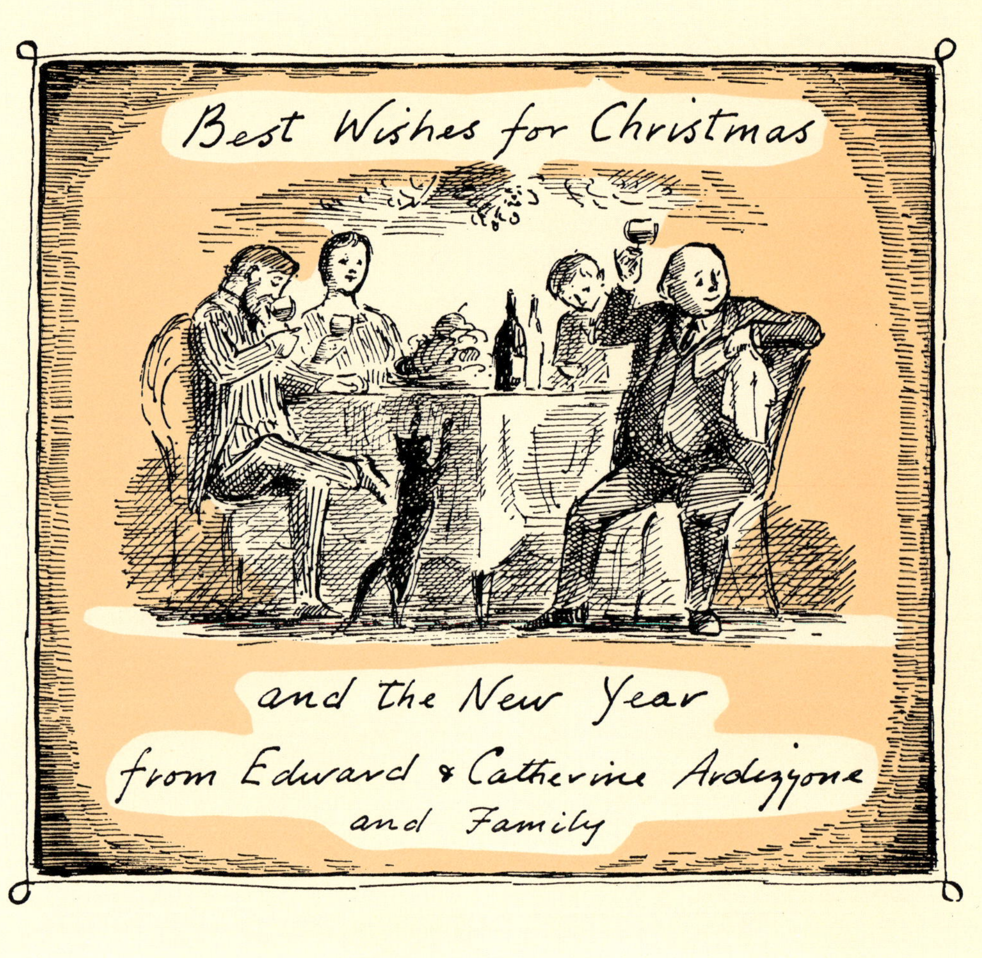
Best Wishes for Christmas
and the New Year
from Edward & Catherine Ardizzone
and Family

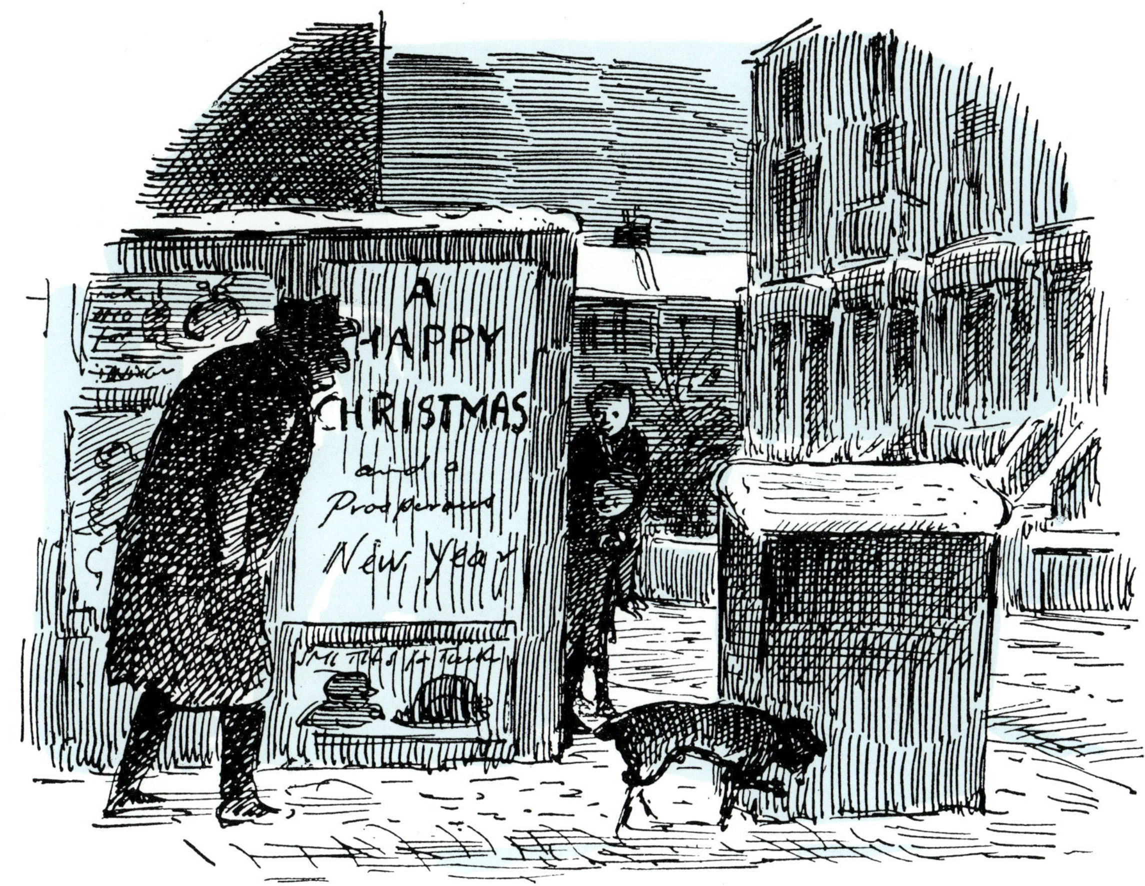

from Catherine & Edward Ardizzone

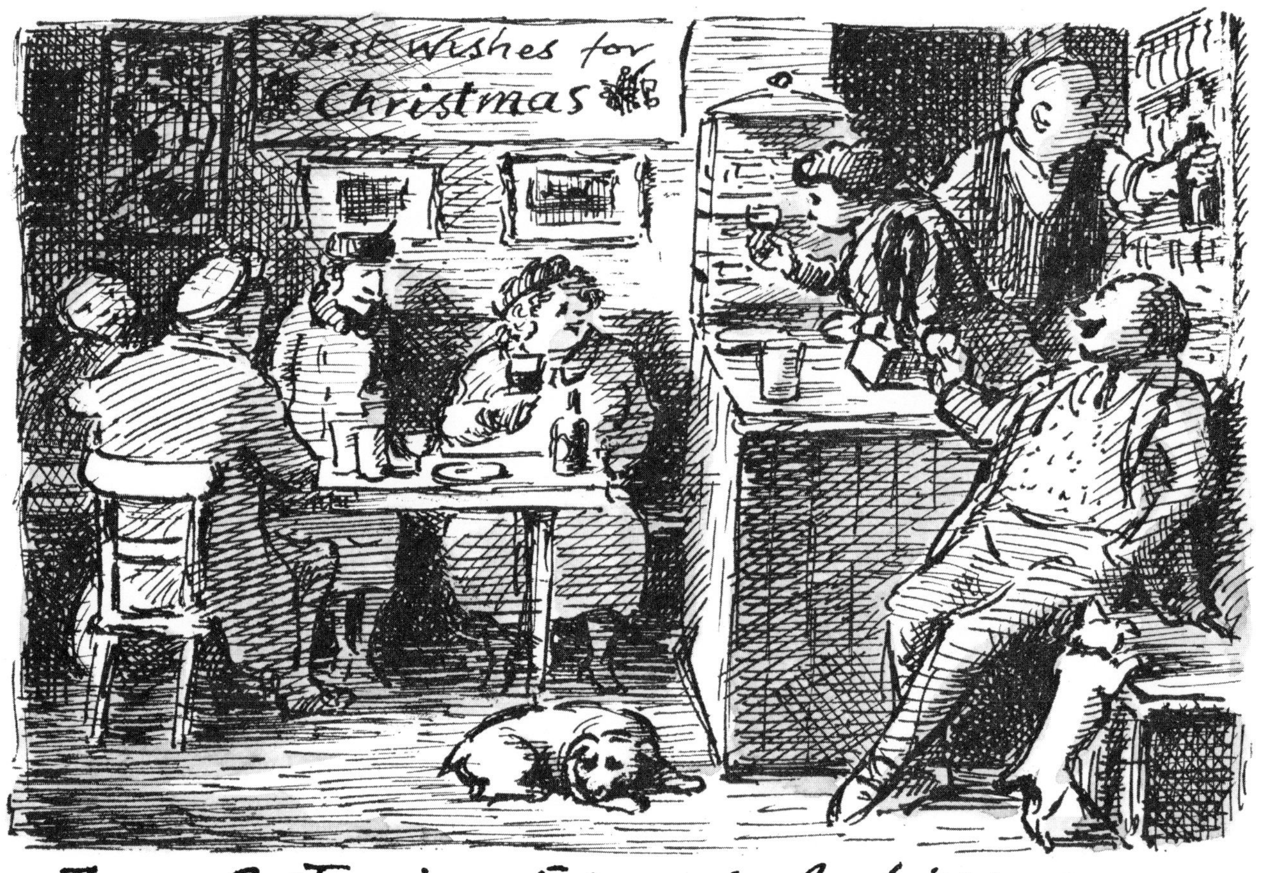

From Catherine & Edward Ardizzone —

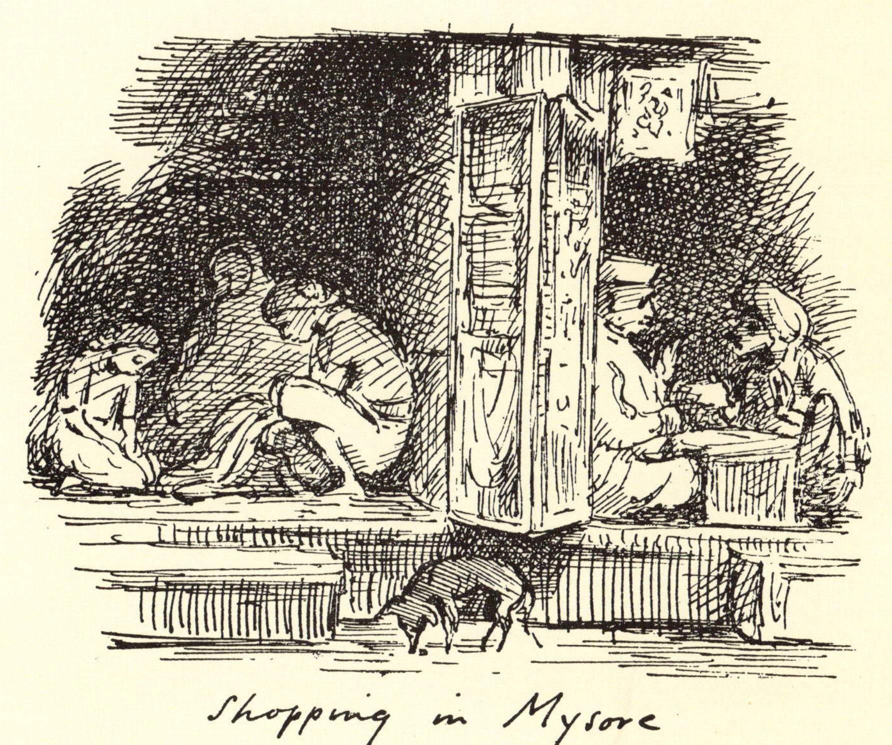

With best Wishes
for
Christmas
and the
New Year
from
Catherine
and
Edward
Ardizzone

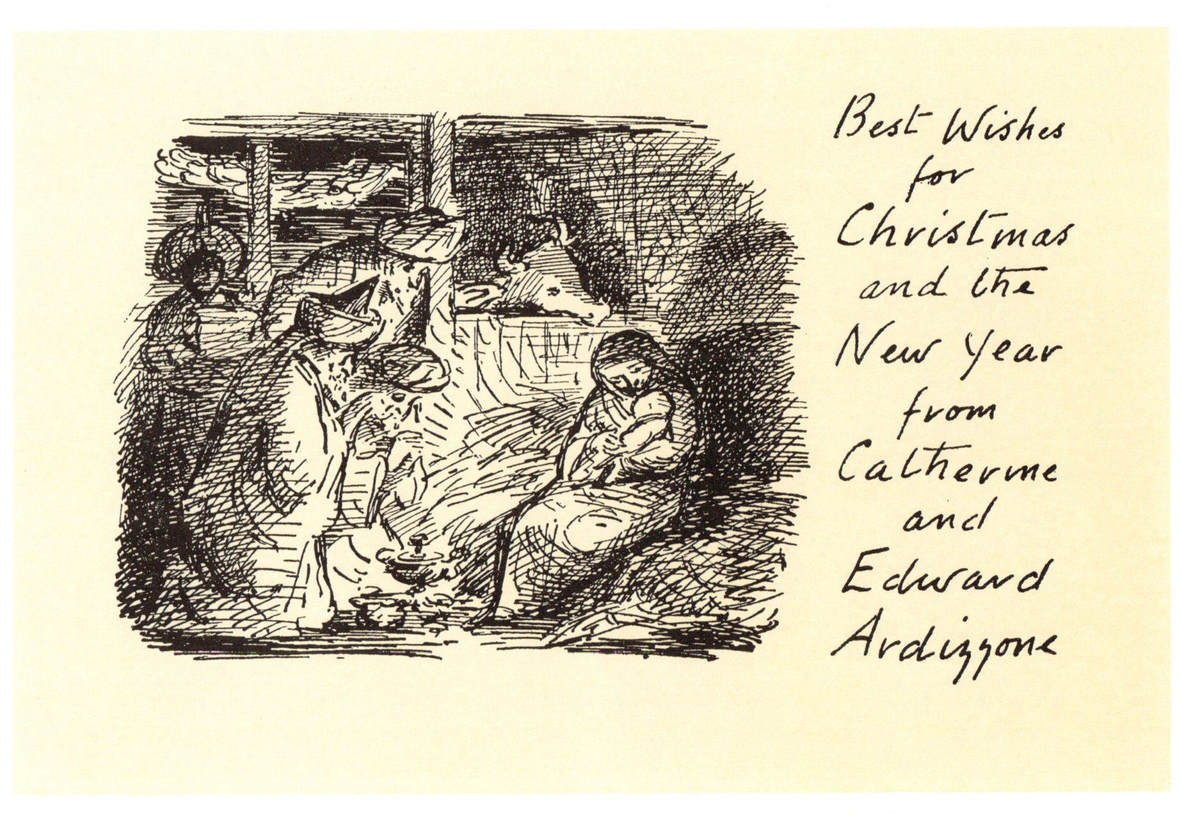

For the Christmas of 1952, we received Ted's 'shopping in Mysorc' card. This was inspired by his visit there in November of that year for UNESCO during the six months he worked for them. This, in turn, inspired my father to reminisce about his own experiences in India during the Second World War while he was in ENSA.

Another card which belongs to the same period, being in the same style and size, is of a nativity scene. This religious flavour seems out of keeping with his usual subjects but it was around this time, during the early 50's, that Ardizzone began work on a number of oil panels for the altar piece of the Carmelite Church of Faversham, Kent.

Life was simple at Elgin Avenue. I remember, from my many visits, the mid-day meals, which always consisted of good basic fare: wine, bread and cheese eaten at a large table in the centre of the first floor room in front of the fire place and the gilded Victorian mantelpiece mirror. The walls were covered in paintings, in some places edge to edge, and the house was always full of visitors. This same first floor room had French windows and two big sash windows next to which was a one foot high wooden dais. Here Ardizzone set up his stool and drawing board; the dais had been a present and proved to be ideal: 'It kept Ted out of the draughts.' He spent the rest of his London days working on this throne, happily surrounded by his family [see cover illustration].

The house was divided into two: the top floors were occupied by Gabriel and Betty and their sons Christopher and Anthony, while Ted and Catherine and their children, Christianna, Philip and Nicholas filled the rest of the house.

The card we received in Broadstairs for Christmas 1955 is of carol singers outside 130 Elgin Avenue. As Catherine said, looking again at the card recently, 'It wasn't so sleek as this, but still!' This, like his other cards, is both a record of a period in London, and an idealization. It evokes the rather stark and grimy terraced house offset by flattering trimmings of fresh, white snow. How rarely did London ever have, or indeed have now, such a clean, snowy and perfect Christmas?! Perhaps Ted's memories of the bad winter of 1946 still lived in his mind.

In Broadstairs when this card arrived it had pride of place on the mantelpiece. I remember my father placing it firmly in the very centre!

I recall that one year my father also decided to make his own Christmas cards. He painted in oils on thick, strong cartridge paper – mostly a Christmas rose motif – making about 40 cards. But after sending one to his brother and one

to Ted and family he kept the rest; we still have them today.

Christmas is an important time for all people but it is especially magical for children. We in Broadstairs had the same traditional Christmas that my father had had as a boy. It followed the old German customs in many respects. On Christmas morning the stockings of my sister, my brothers and myself would be filled. Every year we would keep awake as late as we could and sit in the dark waiting to catch Father Christmas at his task, but we always fell asleep only to wake later to find the stockings filled with toys and with the traditional Clementine oranges and nuts in the toe. Going downstairs we would find my mother had already put the turkey in the oven. Then off to church. We always went to St. Peter's church because of its splendid Norman nave. Although our parish was that of Holy Trinity, Broadstairs, my father preferred St. Peter's; he loved it particularly for its fine graveyard with a view over the Thanet. It was here that he wished to be buried, and here that indeed he lies, buried in 1969, joined by my mother ten years later.

After church we would walk excitedly home to our Christmas lunch, the high point of the day and the height of luxury for us: paper hats, turkey and sprouts, and then Christmas pudding aflame with brandy. Lunch over, there came the traditional walk to Joss Bay while my poor mother and sister were left behind to wash up!

It wasn't until the afternoon, at about four o'clock, that we were allowed into the room with the Christmas tree and presents. Before that my father busied himself with the tree and the presents, lighting the candles and decorating

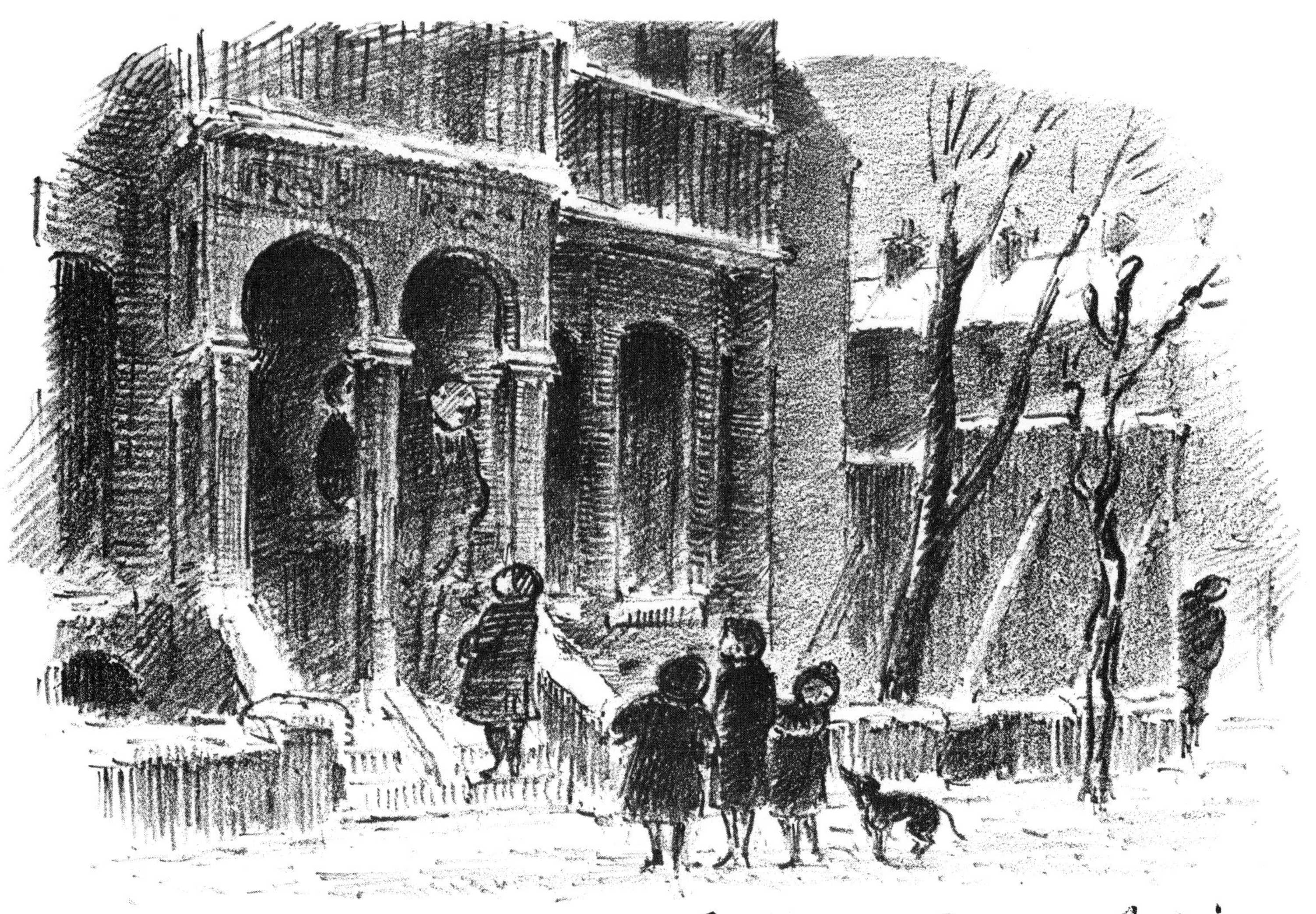

Best Wishes for Christmas from Catherine & Edward Ardizzone

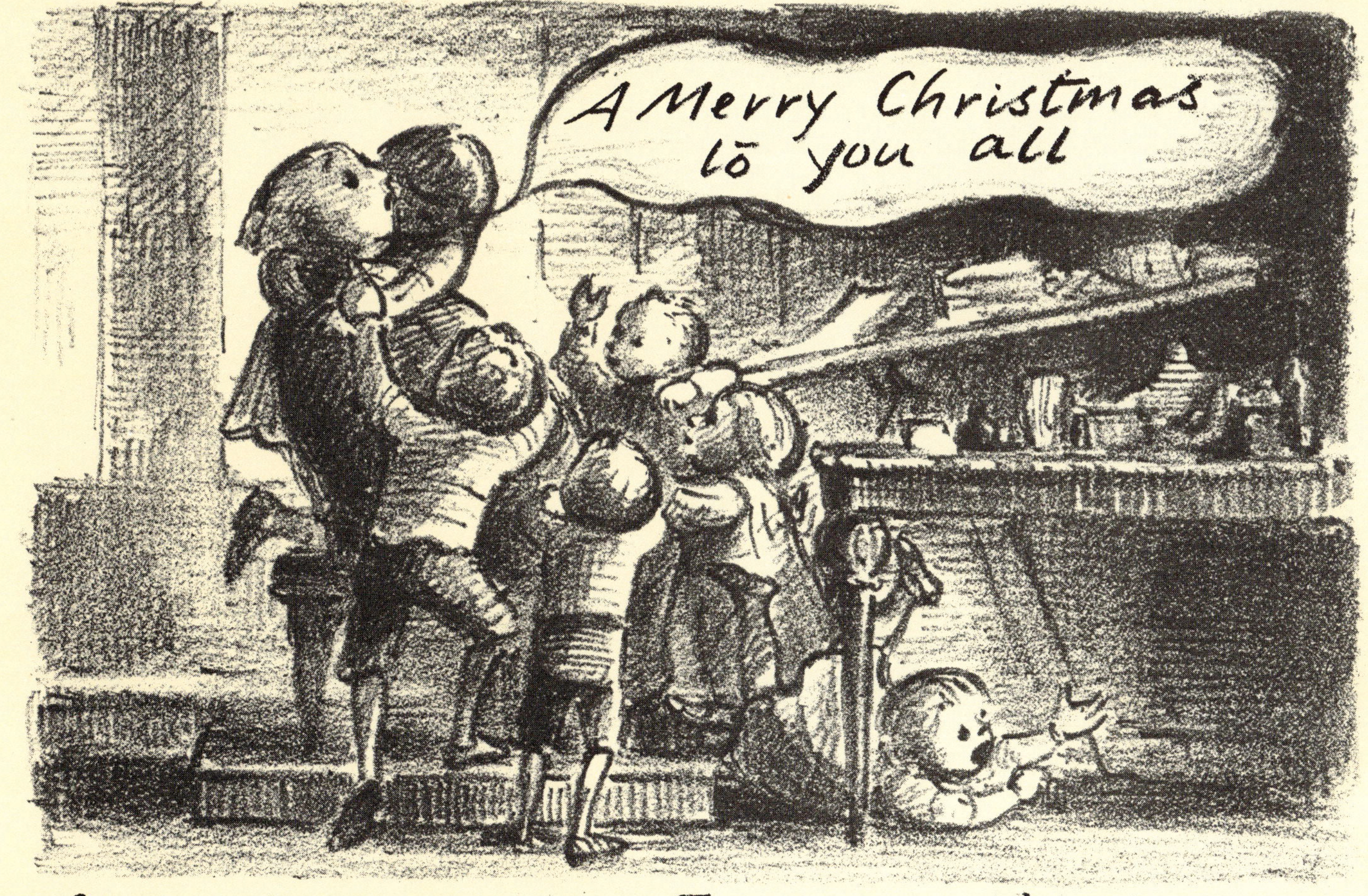

from Catherine & Edward Ardizzone

your picture looks splendid in a black & gold frame   Ted

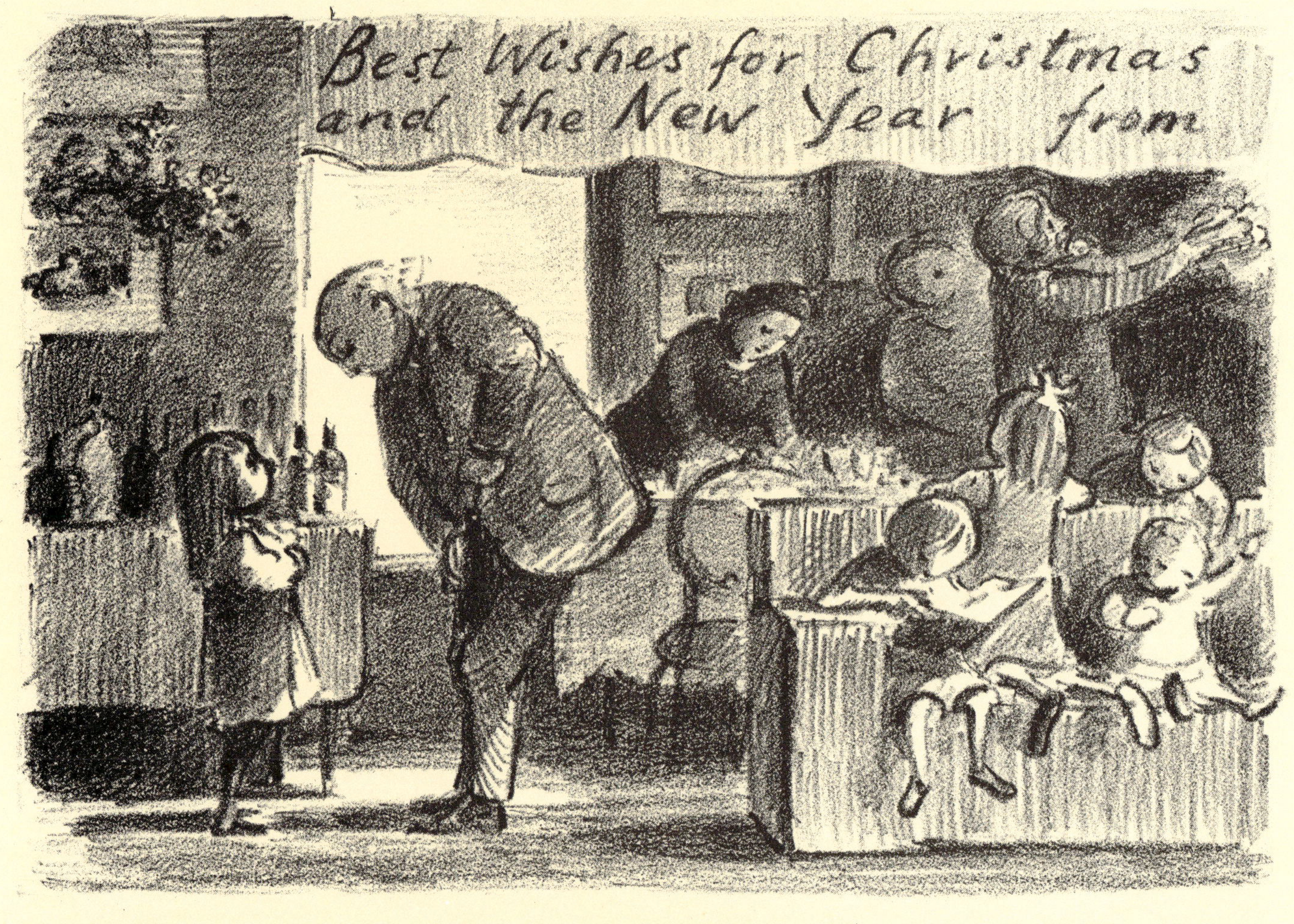

Catherine + Edward Ardizzone

the room. We children and my mother stood outside the closed door and sang as loud as we could, and eventually he would fling open the door – when he thought we had sung well enough! There before us was the room filled with light: the red glowing warmth of the coal fire and the flickering flames of the candles on the tree, reflecting off the sparkling decorations. After the carols came my father's address: he spoke to us of the years gone by and gave thanks. Only now did he hand out the presents from under and on the tree – and the rest of the evening was spent unwrapping parcels, each of us warm and content within the bosom of the family.

On occasions my grandmother, 'La Maréchale', would come and stay bringing my father's nanny, Adèle, and sometimes we were also joined by members of the Hamnett side of the family – so Christmas was often quite a major family affair.

I recall one Christmas we were struck by drama when the tree went up in flames. This created pandemonium – much to us children's delight! Yet, even after this, my father still insisted on having candles each year.

The next card from the Ardizzones depicts Edward besieged by his clamouring grandchildren. The message on the bottom refers to a painting that he had bought from my father; in later years Ted was always extremely generous in buying some of his work and his support was a great encouragement to my father [p.30].

The Ardizzone Christmas differed somewhat from ours. They would start their day with stockings for all the children at No. 130. Then Ted's daughter, Christianna and her husband John Clemence who lived in Richmond, would come up with their children; and Ted's son, Philip and his wife Aingelda would sometimes be staying. After the stocking ritual the candles on the tree would be lit – this would be around midday – and everyone would open their parcels. Meanwhile the Christmas dinner was cooking, and by the time the great feast was ready the children had opened all their presents and were, hopefully, playing happily and contentedly with their new toys.

On page 31 you see Ted opening the wine as Joanna, one of the grandchildren, looks on with interest. On the sofa, engrossed in a new book is Quentin, with Damian next to him and Sara looking over from behind. Catherine puts the final touches to the table, Christianna lends a hand while Philip adjusts the mistletoe.

Reminiscing about those large family Christmases, Catherine added that invariably after the great midday feast one or two of the children would fall asleep, curled up under the tree – 'it was enchanting – they were just exhausted with too many things all in one day.'

Christmas was the one time when the Ardizzones did not go to the pub; it was very much a time for the family. But on the rare occasion when all the children had gone to bed early enough, Ted, Philip and Gabriel might pop out for a quick drink.

In the majority of his Christmas cards Ardizzone made a point of recording local landmarks. In this card three young children stand poised to pelt Ted with snowballs as he rounds the corner. Behind them, in typical tongue-in-cheek humour, Ardizzone's Santa Claus holds up a bottle of beer or stout as an advertisement for the festive season; his expression is decidedly cheeky. In the background is the

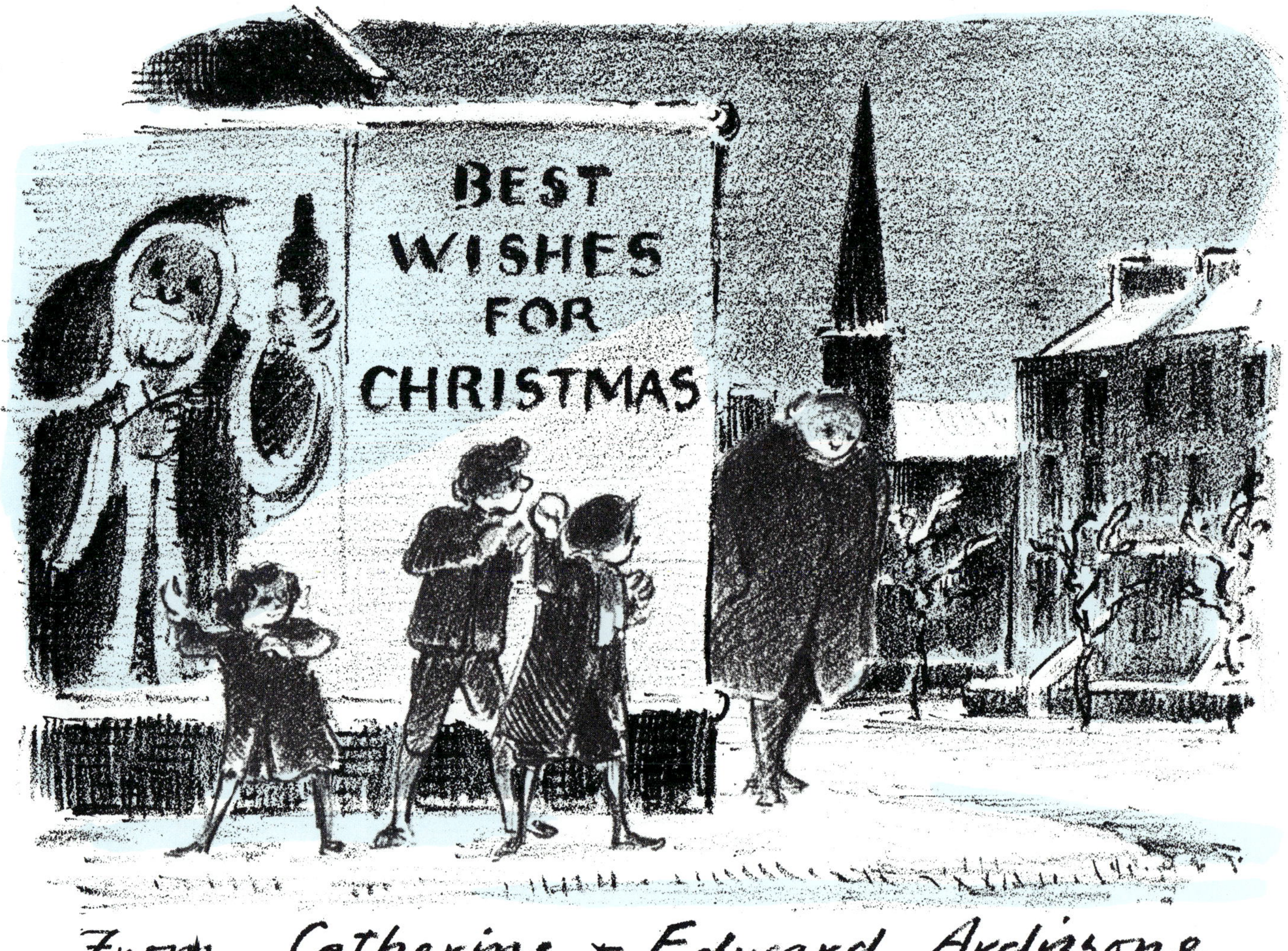

From Catherine & Edward Ardizzone

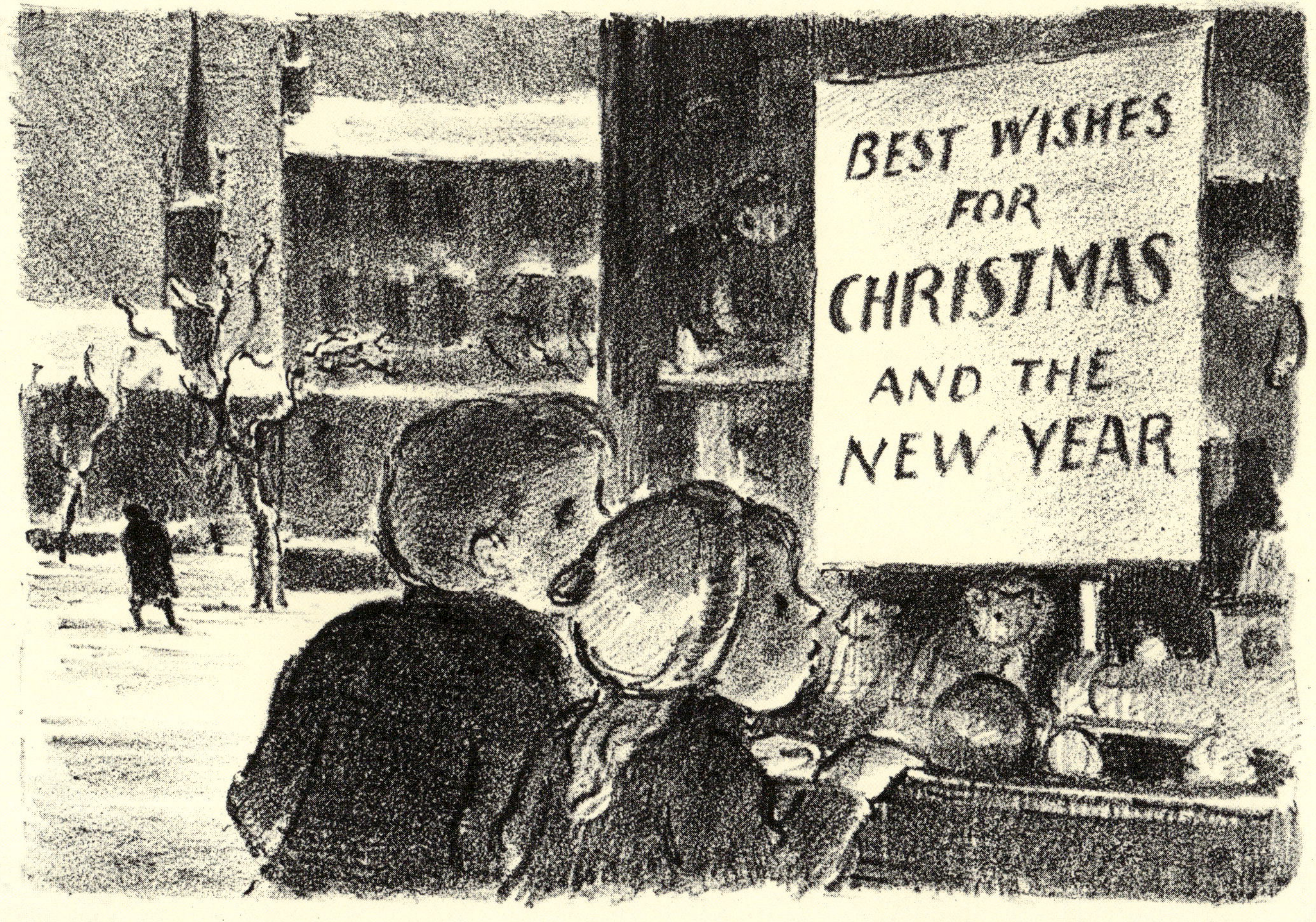

From Catherine & Edward Ardizzone —
with love   1963

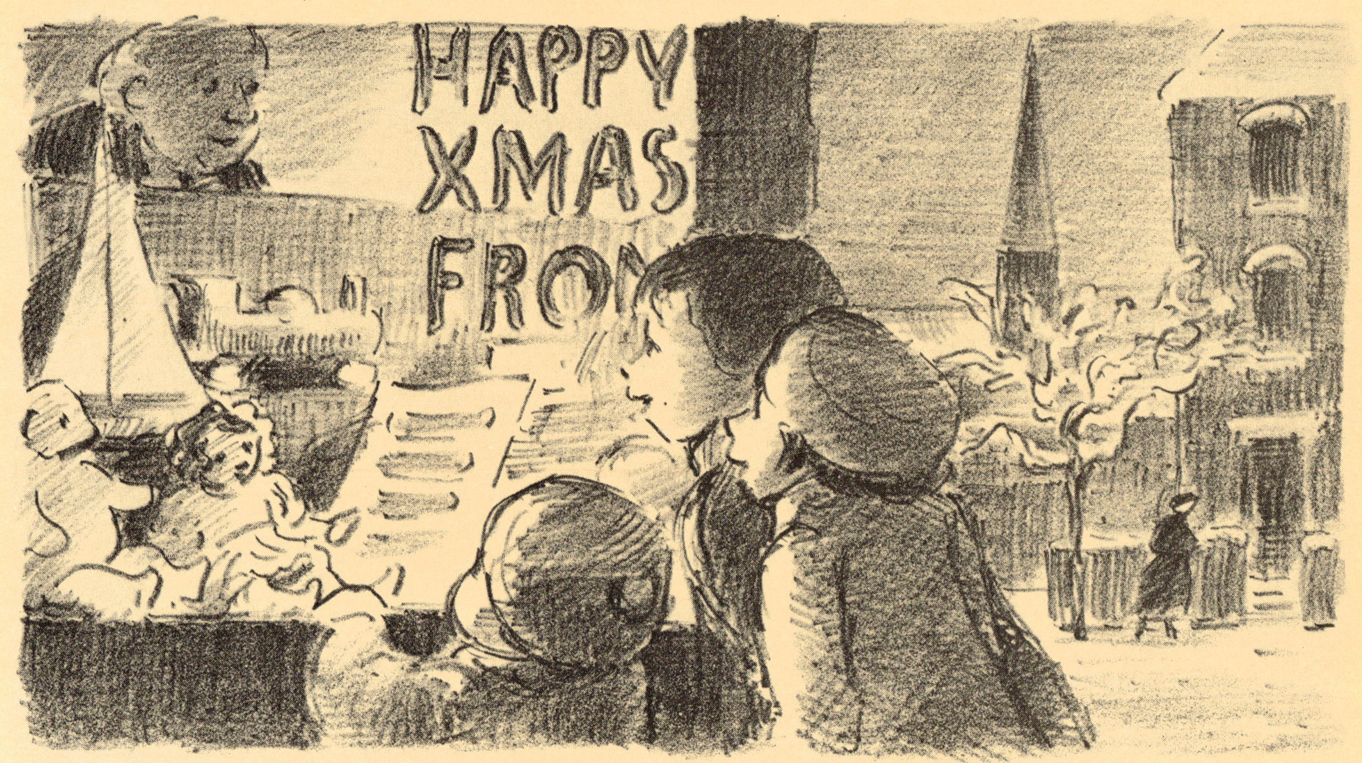

Catherine & Edward Ardizzone

Happy New Year and love

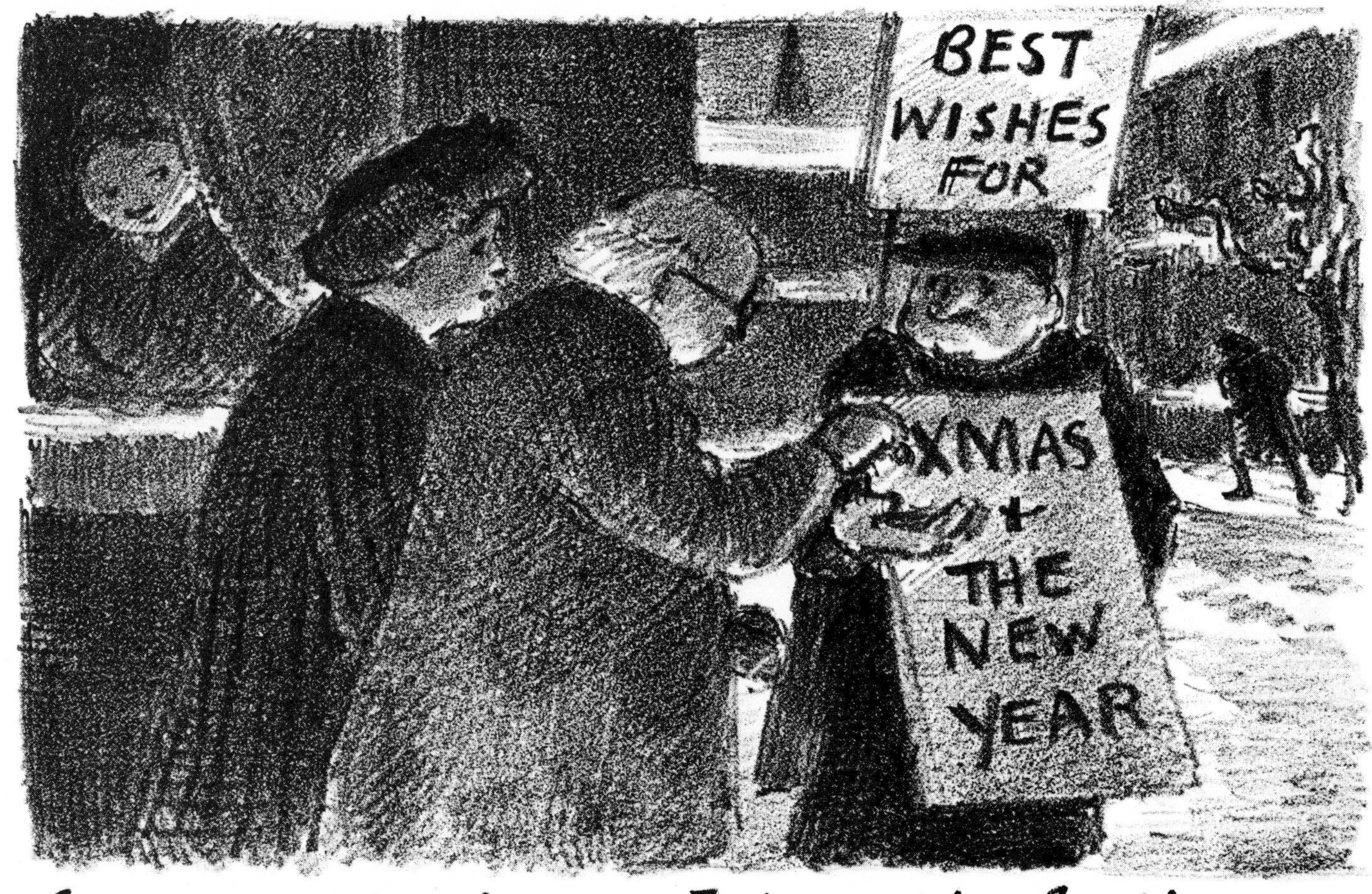

from Catherine & Edward Ardizzone

spire of St. Peter's Church, Elgin Avenue. The familiar profile of this church appears in several of the cards, but the church itself, built in 1870, was pulled down in 1975 due to declining congregations and structural damage.

The card for Christmas 1963 featuring two children absorbed by the goodies in the toy-shop window, shows another view of St. Peter's Church, and the next card is a variation on the same theme. A further card of Catherine and Ted shows, in the background, another distant view of the spire [pp. 34–6].

In 1956, the Ardizzones bought an old Riley. It was very small, but nonetheless, 'you can see about 99 people squeezed into the back,' Catherine jokes. 'We began by having an Isetta. It was a little round thing with no nose and the gears were terribly close to one another. You opened the front up, climbed in and drove away.' Ted adored the car but should never really have driven as he had by then had an operation for cataracts [p. 38].

Talk of the car reminded Catherine of my father's visits: 'He used to come and see us quite a bit at Elgin Avenue and spend the night. It was so funny to see your father and Ted in the bubble car – fit to burst! And Ted I look upon as the worst driver under the sun. He used to drive Augustin to Victoria to put him on a train to Broadstairs. He told me that everybody was so nice to Augustin – you know, the policemen and porters obviously all knew him; they used to greet him and put him on the train and send him home.'

Ardizzone will perhaps be best remembered for his illustrated children's books, especially the Tim series which he both wrote and illustrated. These books made wonderful Christmas gifts for children. They told the story of the continuing adventures of a young lad, Tim, who lived on the South coast and whose escapades usually involved 'going to sea' and 'messing about on boats', salty tales told by friendly sea captains, faithful dogs and his young friend Lucy. The Tim books also belong to the period of life at Elgin Avenue. Catherine recalls the great satisfaction he got from creating these books but also his sudden decision nevertheless, to stop illustrating and to devote himself solely to his painting:

'He adored illustrating, loved it. In the old days he used to do about eight illustrations in a day, but by the last book he worked on – this was after he broke his leg, and he must have been in pain most of the time – he would do only two a day and prepare one for the next morning . . . He said to me quite suddenly, "I'm never going to sign another contract. After this I'm going to paint – and for love." This was in 1979 when he was half way through the last book he did; and the book he never finished: *Ardizzone's English Fairy Tales*. But he did love doing it.'

In 1966 Ardizzone bought a cottage, No. 5 Vine Cottages, in Rodmersham Green, Kent. This is when the Christmas cards start to acquire a country flavour. They now depict walks down snow covered lanes, the element of cosy warmth coming no longer from a cheery pub interior but from the lighted windows of the snug little cottage at the end of the lane. The snowball fight between rival village gangs of boys also has a rural setting [pp. 40, 41].

A few of the cards deviate from the family themes. Reminders of Ardizzone's profession as a painter, they have a lighthearted, witty charm all their own even if they convey less of the particular atmosphere of snow and cheer, and the

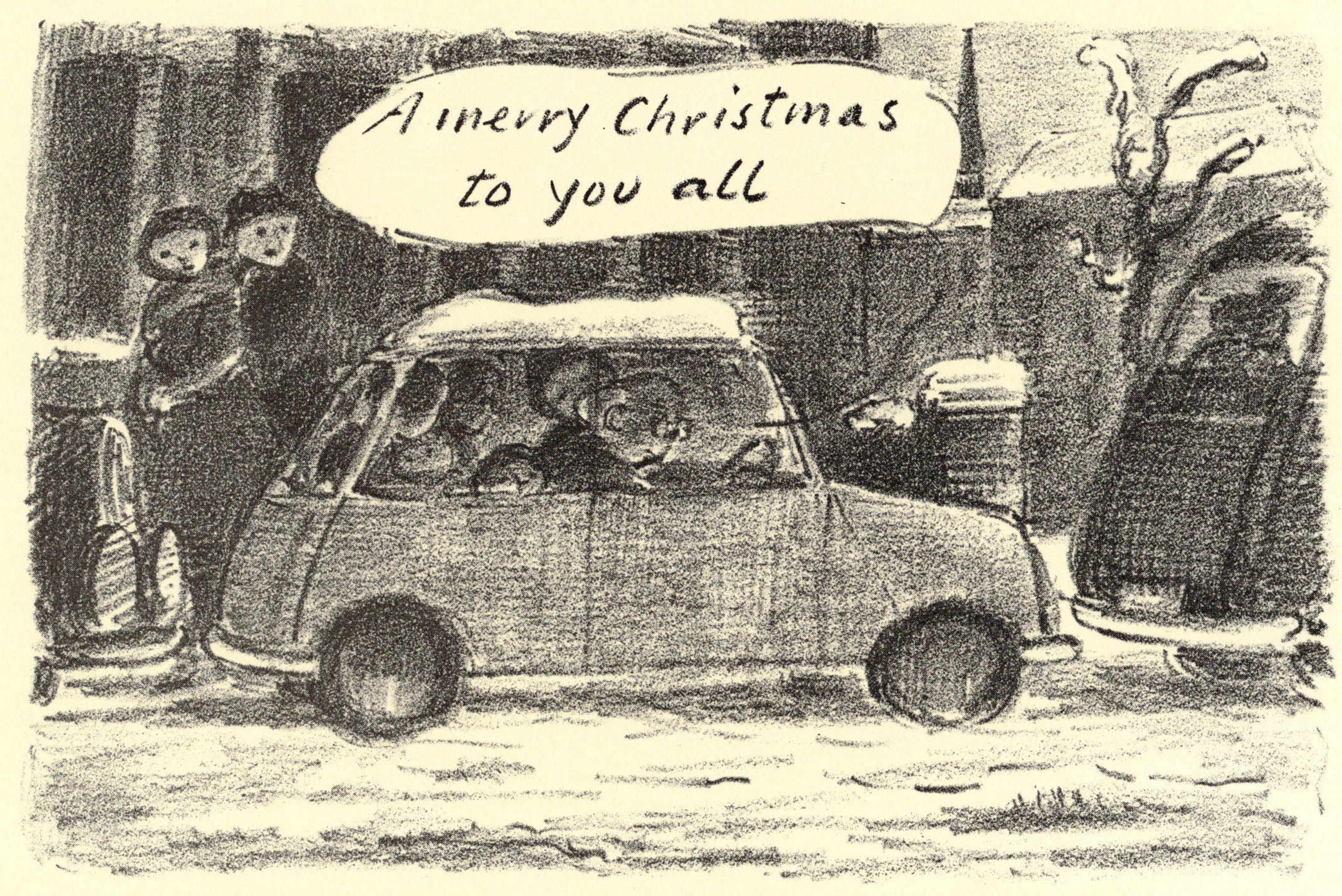

from Catherine & Edward Ardizzone
with love

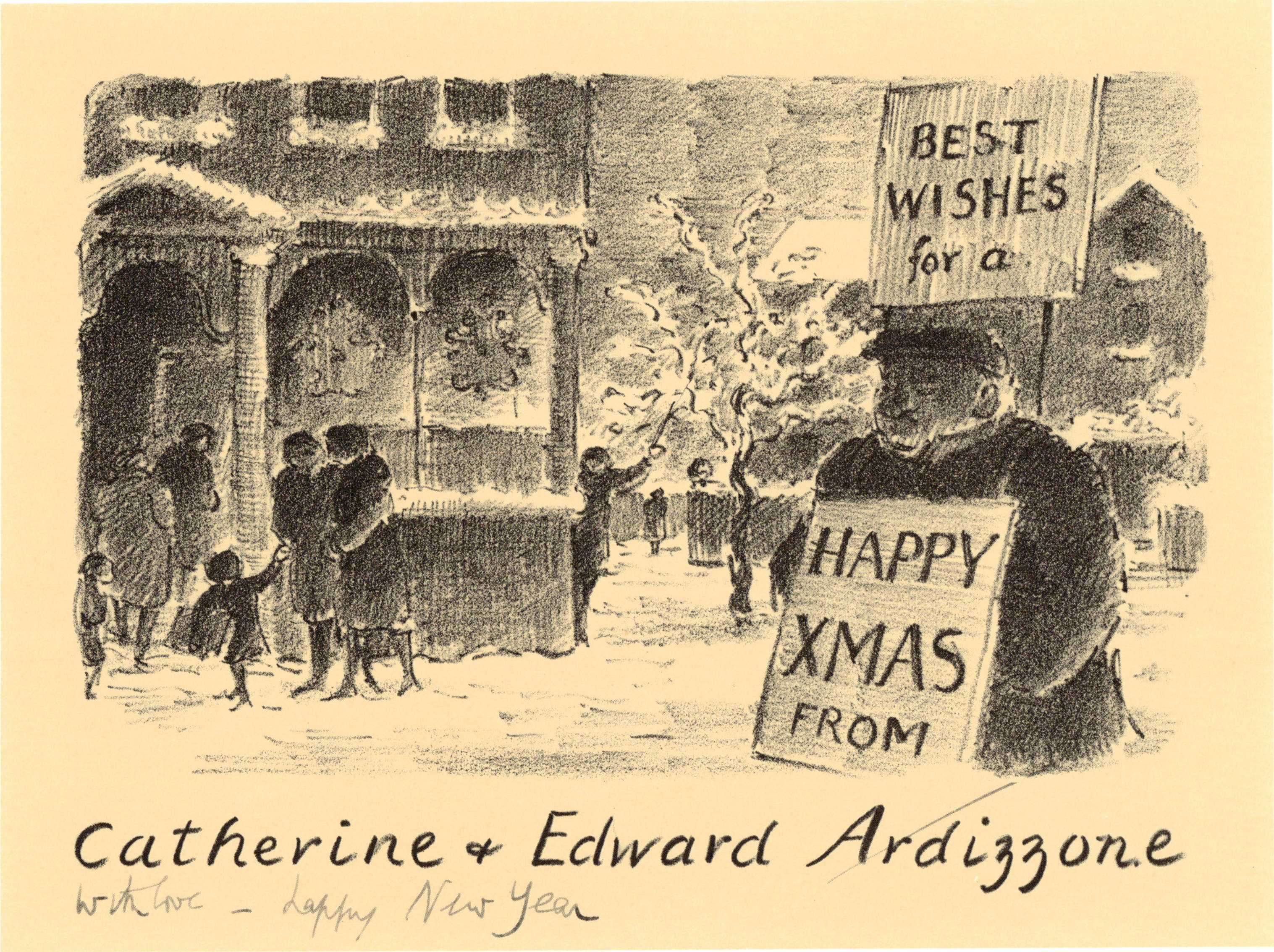

Catherine & Edward Ardizzone

with love — happy New Year

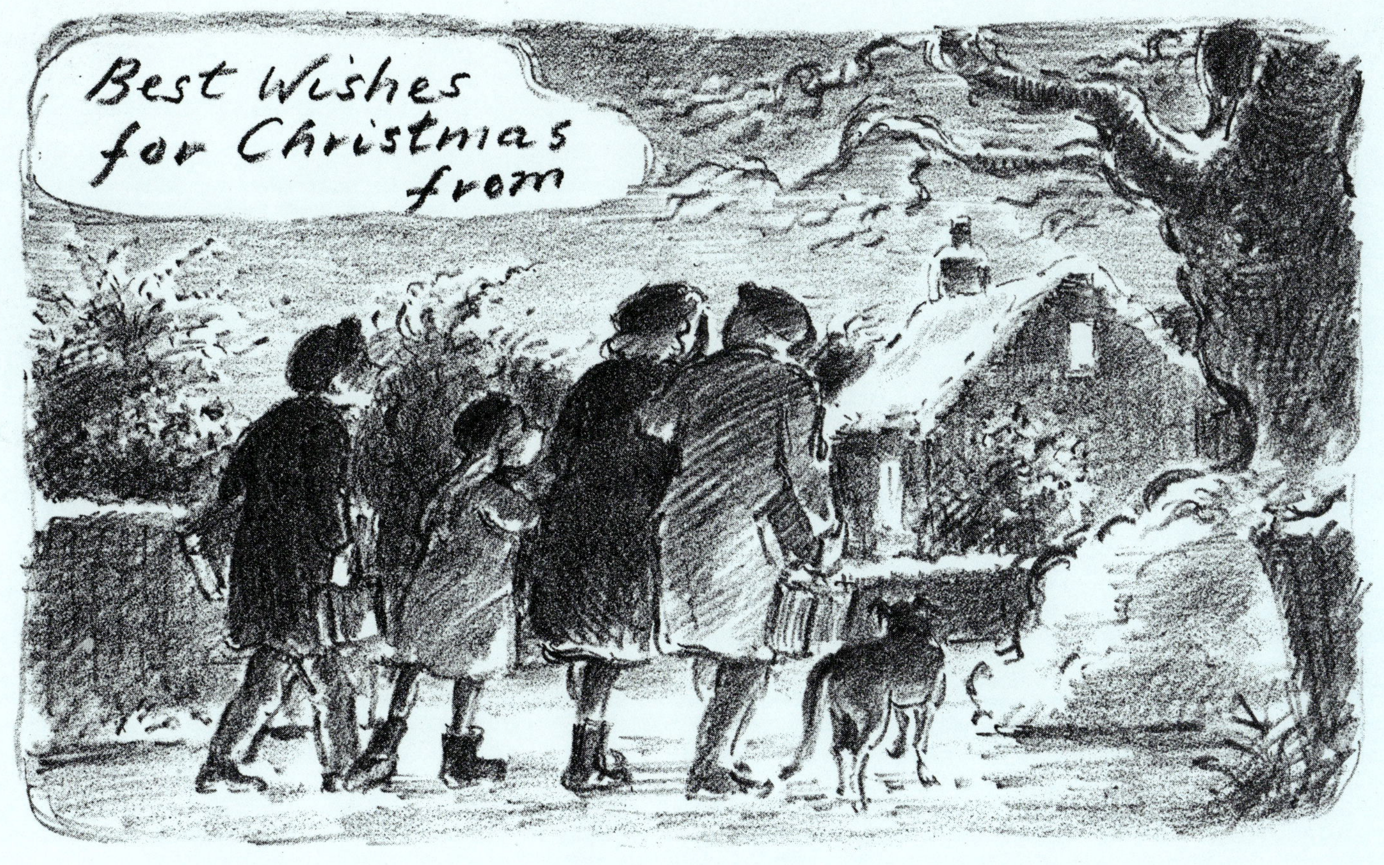

Catherine & Edward Ardizzone

With love —

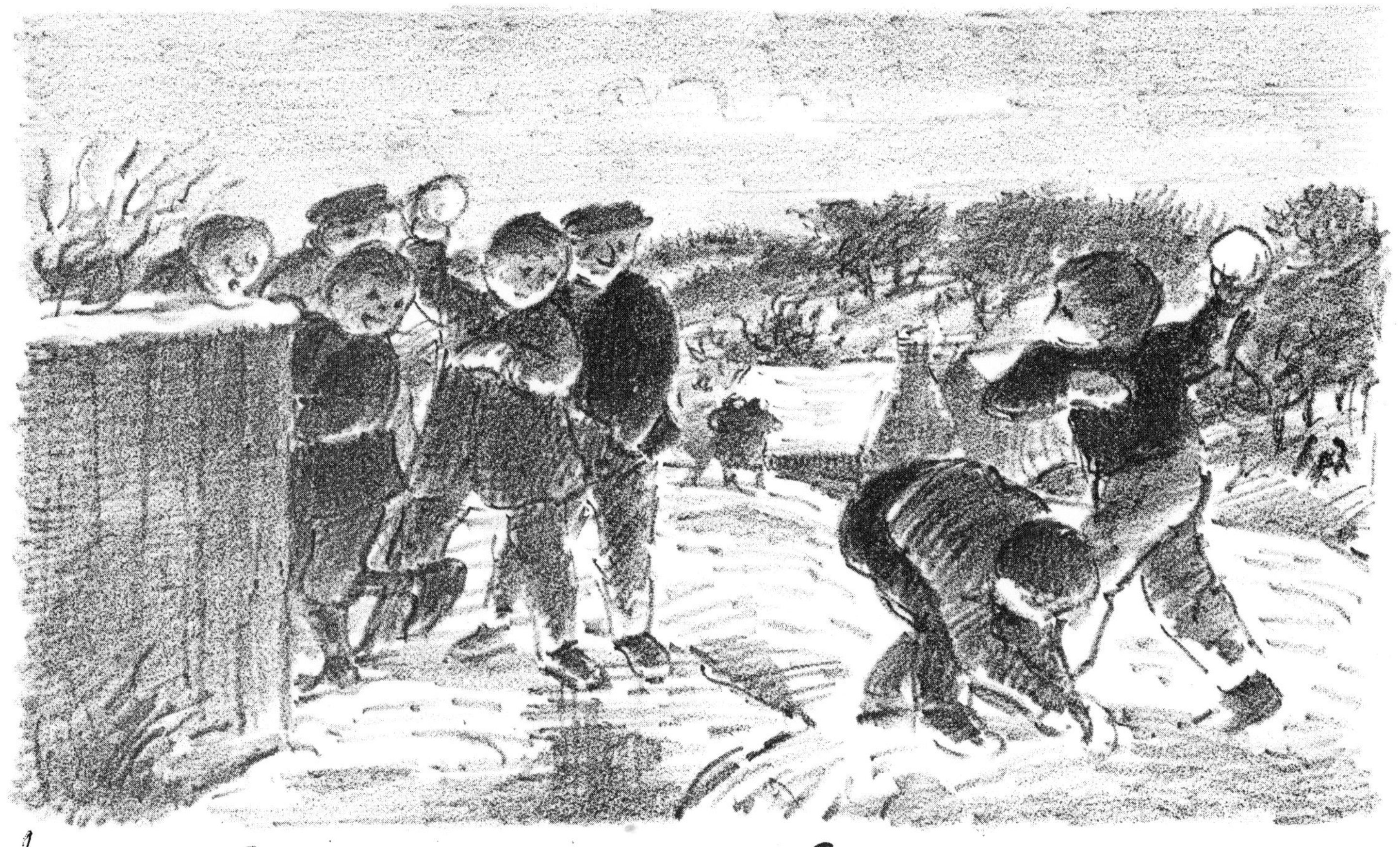

Love & Best Wishes for Christmas
from Catherine & Edward Ardizzone

Catherine & Edward Ardizzone

cosy warmth of family life that he built up so success-fully over the years in the main body of Christmas cards.

Time moved on. My father had a one-man show at the Upper Grosvenor Galleries in 1965, but he visited London less and less. Ted's visits to Broadstairs, however, continued as always. My father painted on in his garage studio until his death in 1969. At the funeral a huge bouquet of bright yellow flowers stood out: it was from Ted. My mother stayed on in Bradstow Way until her own death in 1979 and during all this time we still received the annual Ardizzone card come Christmas time. Now the Christmases, whether in Broadstairs or in London, included grandchildren as well, and they too came to love the Ardizzone card, which, following the ritual established by my father, would always be placed in the centre of the mantelpiece.

In 1972 Ted and Catherine decided to leave Elgin Avenue permanently and settle in Vine Cottages. Although the cottage seemed small after the more generous rooms of their London home, Ted had had a studio built in the back garden which gave him plenty of space to continue his work.

By now, though, the Christmas cards were reproductions of illustrations from his books. Sadly, he did no more special cards, but Christmas greetings were still sent out to family and friends [pp. 44, 45].

In 1978 I took my sons to visit the Ardizzones at Vine Cottages. Warm and generous as ever he allowed them to watch him at work. His love of the young had not abated as he had grown older and he made a drawing of my son, Patrick, while Patrick drew him. Unfortunately Patrick's drawing has been lost, but Ted's drawing of Patrick, head bent intensely over his sheet of paper, will always be kept.

I was always aware of how important for my father was the contact with both his close friend and with the London he loved, that Ardizzone's Christmas cards provided. Through him I also came to look forward eagerly to their arrival every December and to cherish them long after the festive season was past. Their importance for both of us extended well beyond their role as Christmas greetings. For this reason I kept them each year. Not all, alas, have remained; things disappear with time.

Looking back over the years of cards certain themes stand out. A constant one is the friendly interiors of Ted's local pubs. The other major one is that of the intimacy and enjoyment of family life. All the cards have a gentle sympathy to them – their humour is never cruelly mocking, even when the witty touch is more overt, such as the reindeer spooking the lady drinkers and the Christmas message painted in the presence of the classically draped nude [pp. 46, 47].

Above all Ardizzone depicted in these cards what he saw about him everyday: the local streets, the terraced London houses, the landmarks and life of the neighbourhood. It is rare for an artist to take the unpicturesque, the mundane details of an undramatic life, and make of them something of such charm and pleasure to others, even to those for whom such details could have had no direct meaning. Ardizzone's unselfconscious and spontaneous approach make of these cards an unusual and touching record of Maida Vale and of a London now forever changed by the advance of time.

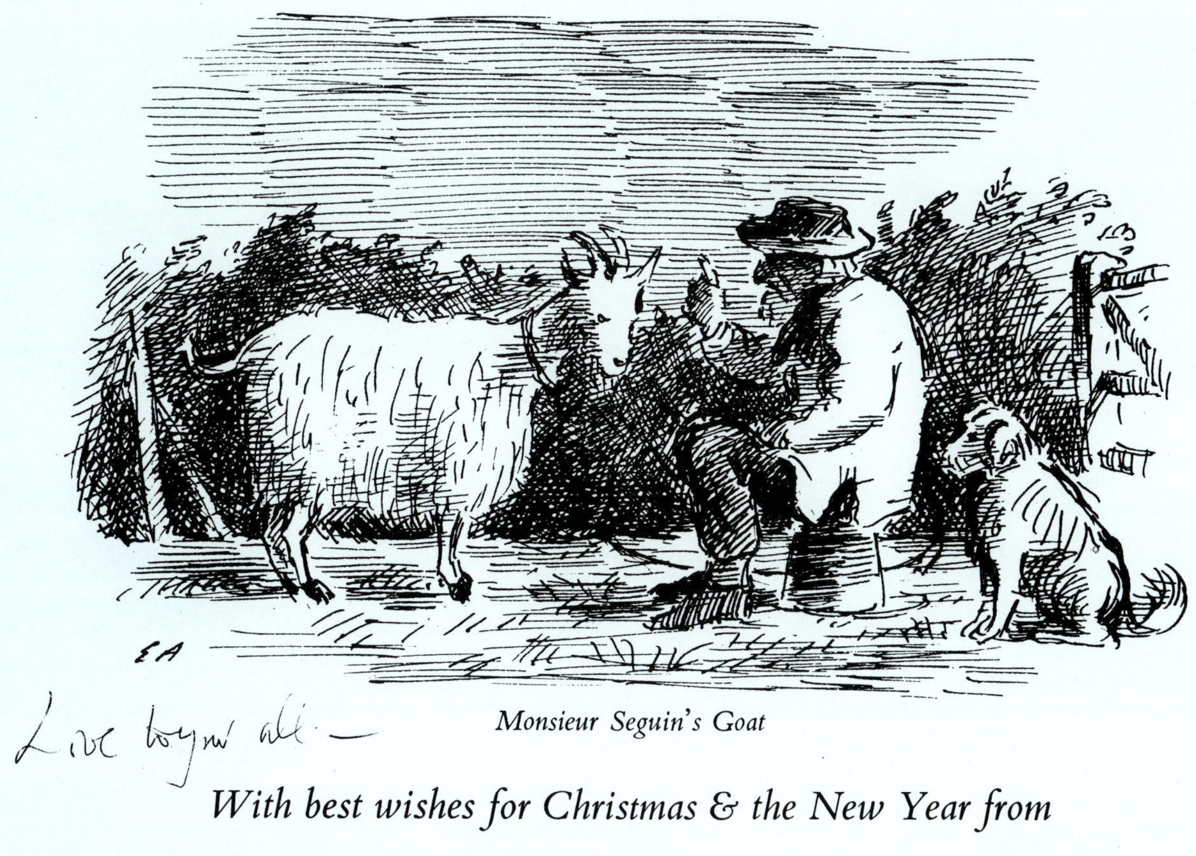

Monsieur Seguin's Goat

With best wishes for Christmas & the New Year from

CATHERINE & EDWARD ARDIZZONE

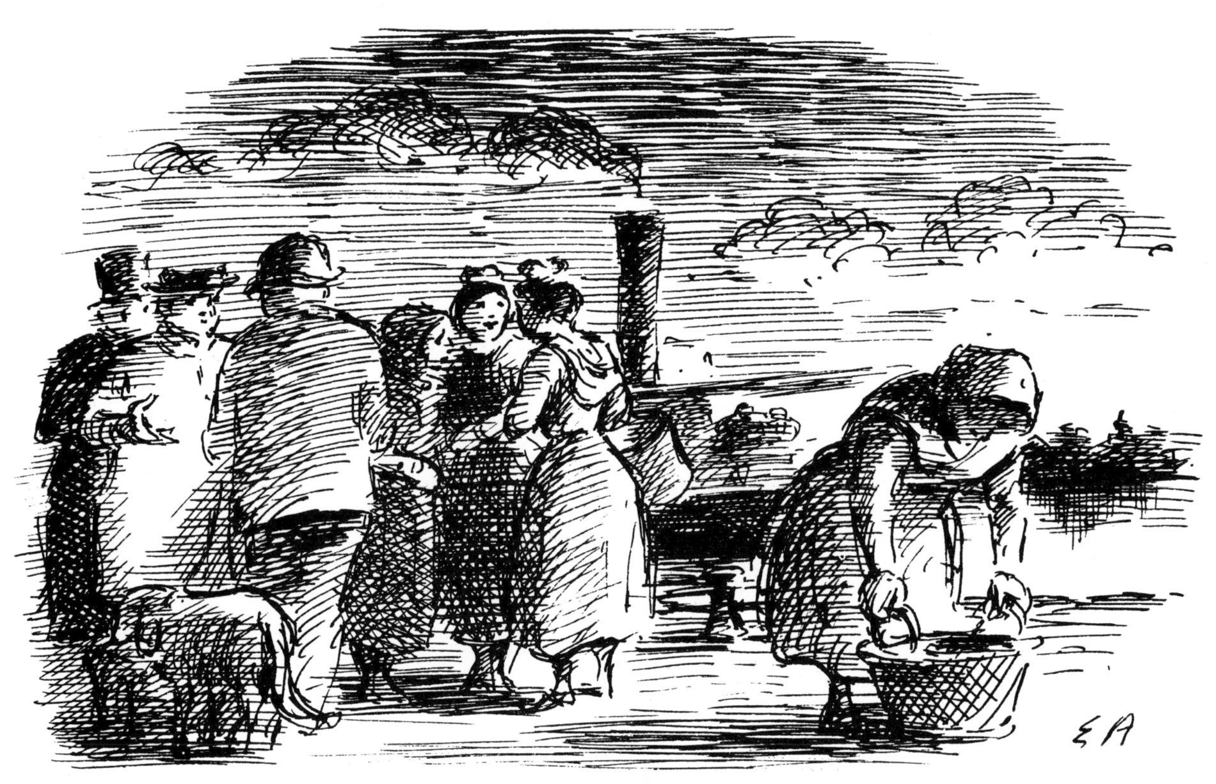

The boat for the Camargue

With best wishes for Christmas & the New Year from

CATHERINE & EDWARD ARDIZZONE

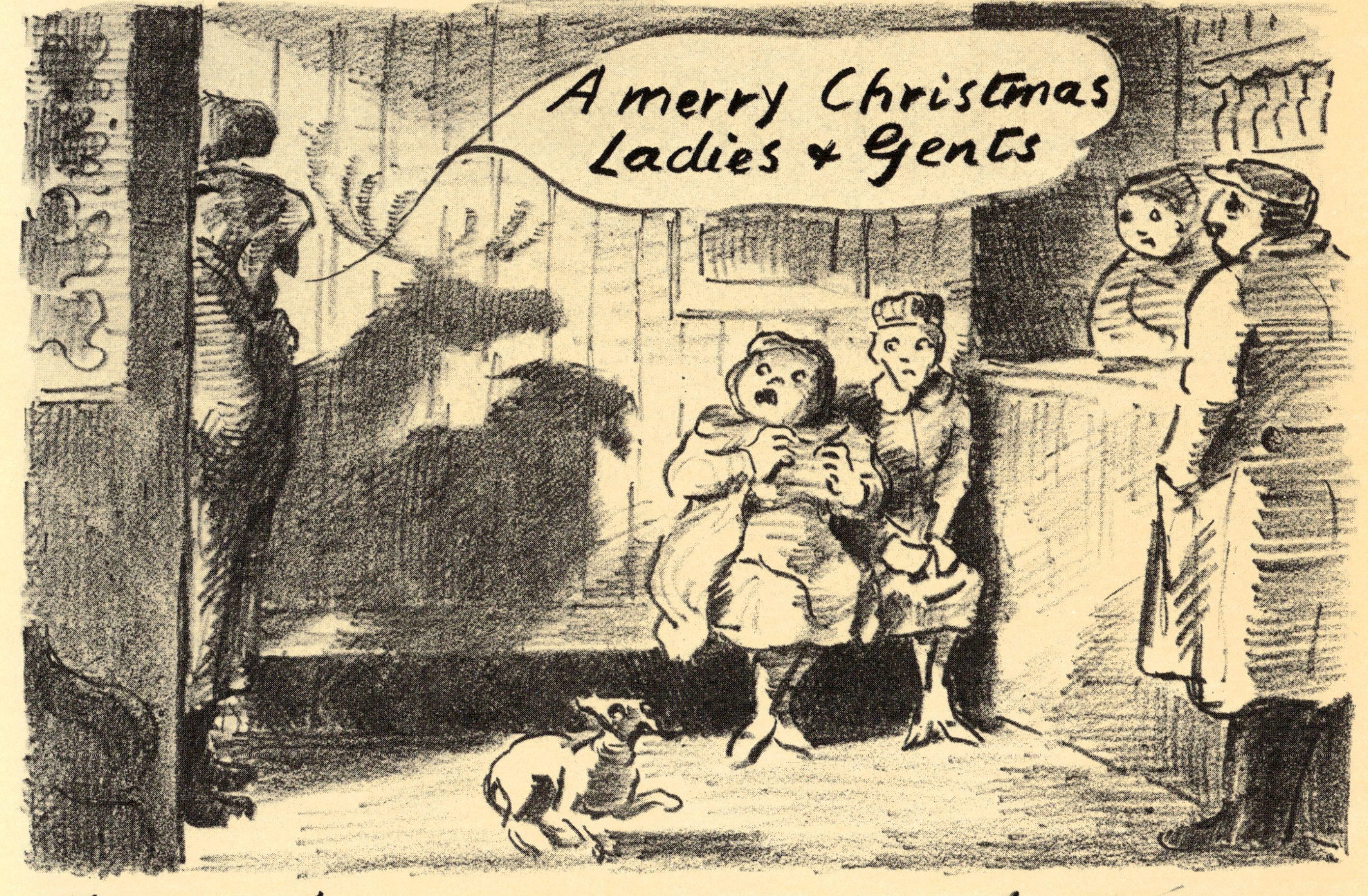

From Catherine & Edward Ardizzone
with love —

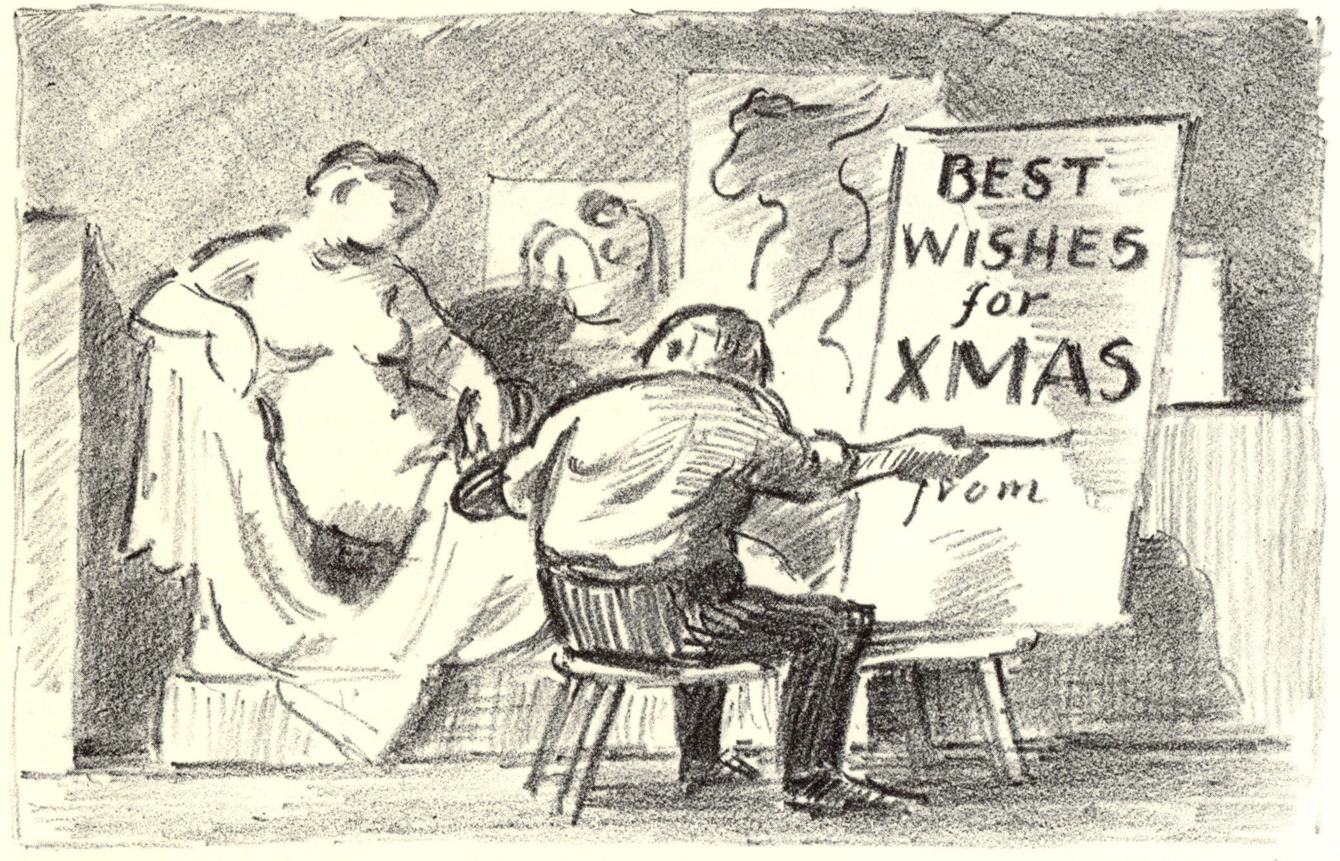

Catherine & Edward Ardizzone
with love —

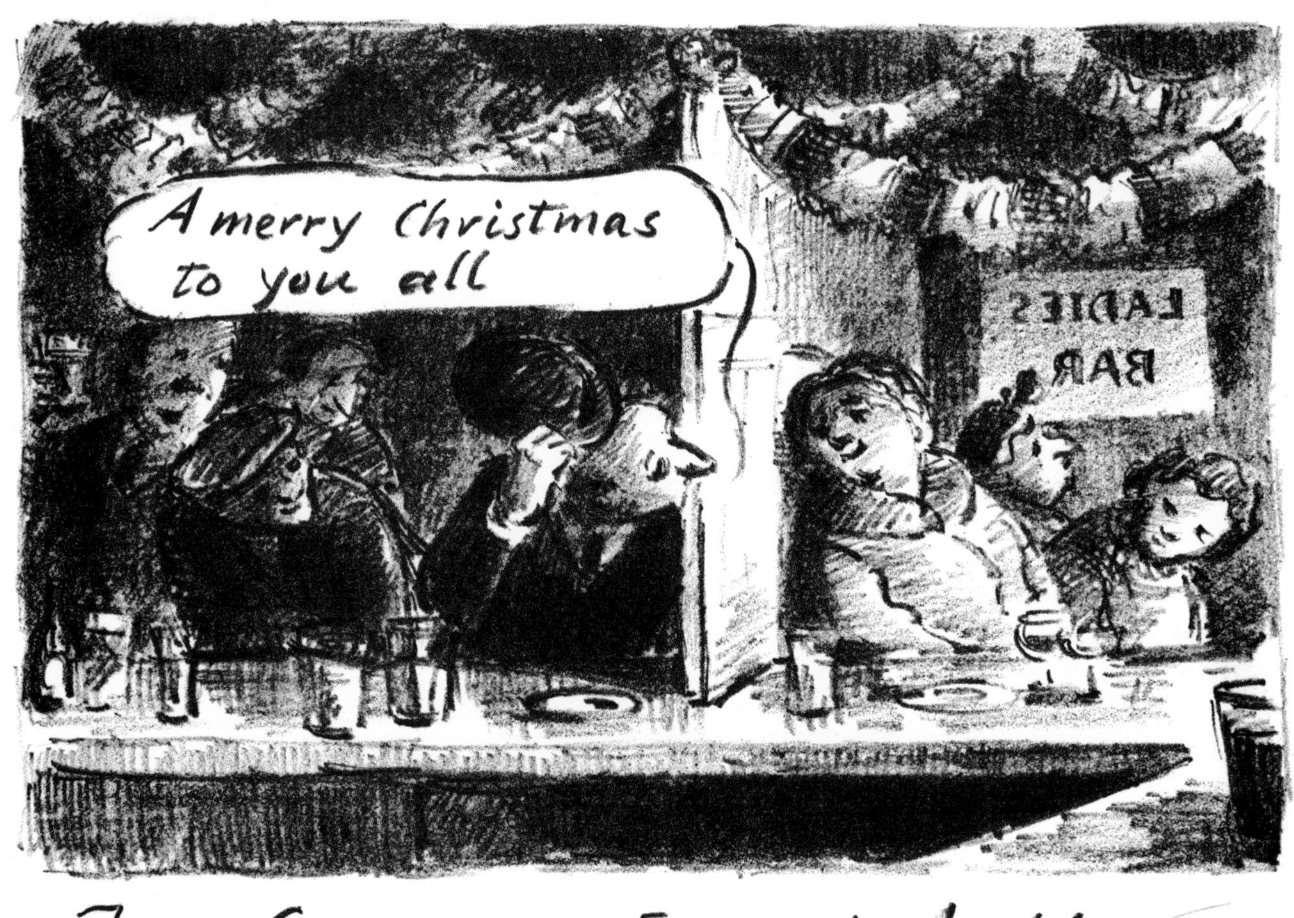

Not since Hogarth and Rowlandson has England had an artist with such a great gift of observation, who so sharply yet with such wit and sympathy and with such artistic skill recorded the simple pleasures of his own life.

Looking back over the years these cards we received allowed us to become part of Ardizzone's world. Especially for my father and mother, but it was also true for me, since I too was invited to share with them something special.